Cambridge Elements

Elements in Environmental Humanities
edited by
Louise Westling
University of Oregon
Serenella Iovino
University of North Carolina at Chapel Hill
Timo Maran
University of Tartu

DESCARTES AND THE NON-HUMAN

Emma Gilby
University of Cambridge

CAMBRIDGE
UNIVERSITY PRESS

Shaftesbury Road, Cambridge CB2 8EA, United Kingdom

One Liberty Plaza, 20th Floor, New York, NY 10006, USA

477 Williamstown Road, Port Melbourne, VIC 3207, Australia

314–321, 3rd Floor, Plot 3, Splendor Forum, Jasola District Centre, New Delhi – 110025, India

103 Penang Road, #05–06/07, Visioncrest Commercial, Singapore 238467

Cambridge University Press is part of Cambridge University Press & Assessment, a department of the University of Cambridge.

We share the University's mission to contribute to society through the pursuit of education, learning and research at the highest international levels of excellence.

www.cambridge.org
Information on this title: www.cambridge.org/9781009617130

DOI: 10.1017/9781009617109

First published 2025

A catalogue record for this publication is available from the British Library

ISBN 978-1-009-61713-0 Hardback
ISBN 978-1-009-61714-7 Paperback
ISSN 2632-3125 (online)
ISSN 2632-3117 (print)

Descartes and the Non-Human

Elements in Environmental Humanities

DOI: 10.1017/9781009617109
First published online: May 2025

Emma Gilby
University of Cambridge

Author for correspondence: Emma Gilby, eg207@cam.ac.uk

Abstract: Descartes features heavily in ecocritical literature. He is often said to dismiss the non-human world as irrelevant and inanimate, and to espouse a harmfully instrumental attitude towards it. This Element goes into detail on the standard picture in circulation, while also outlining an alternative approach that it terms 'ecohistorical'. It aims to offer insights into the seventeenth-century context; and to explain in clear terms what Descartes said, what problems emerge with his account, and why a more precise understanding of these problems can be useful today. Reconsidering Descartes in this light involves extending prior arguments about his treatment of animals to a study of the natural world in general. Early modern narratives about the world's living networks are complex and interesting. When locally salient artefacts, attitudes, ideas, and vocabulary are highlighted, a more nuanced picture emerges, changing the relevance of Descartes for environmental thinking.

Keywords: Descartes, ecocriticism, dualism, mechanism, natural philosophy

ISBNs: 9781009617130 (HB), 9781009617147 (PB), 9781009617109 (OC)
ISSNs: 2632-3125 (online), 2632-3117 (print)

Contents

1 Introduction

Descartes features in much ecocritical literature, and very seldom in a good way. Many readers of this Element – especially those arriving with a prior commitment to the environmental humanities – may therefore find the pairing in its title counterintuitive. Even as ecological criticism diverges widely in the views outlined or the methodologies assumed, it surely gains a fundamental coherence by virtue of its overarching project: the need to tackle environmental catastrophe. It is committed to thinking about how to resituate human cultures within natural systems and landscapes, and imparts an urgent sense of the degradation of our shared planet. Descartes, meanwhile, tends to be viewed as the primary example of a thinker who *dismisses* the non-human world; and it is often held that science and philosophy in the Cartesian tradition have conceived of humans as separate, special, and fundamentally distinct from other entities and processes in the universe. So, why look at him? Historical thinking can, in general, seem inadequate to tackling immediate pressures, and the increasing impossibility of the future. What is the pertinence of early modern intellectual history now?

The starting point for this Element is the wager that it can be of some practical benefit to reconsider what Descartes stands for, not least because he does crop up so very often. 'Dualism' would be one notion often uttered in the same breath as 'Descartes'; or 'the modern subject', or 'selfhood' in general, or 'mastery' or 'domination'. An overarching critique of all these concepts is crucial to the ecocritical project. One summary of the field elaborates as follows: environmental criticism aims itself squarely at the 'presumption to know the natural world scientifically, to manipulate it technologically and exploit it economically, and thereby ultimately to create a human sphere apart from it in a historical process that is usually labeled "progress"' (Heise 2006, 507). This dominating attitude 'strips nature of any value other than as a material resource and commodity and leads to a gradual destruction that may in the end deprive humanity of its basis for subsistence' (507). Such an ideology 'empties human life of the significance it had derived from living in and with nature and alienates individuals and communities from their rootedness in place' (507). And precisely because this is all so clearly the case – because rigidly binary, dualist thinking (us and them, us and that, us and over there) is omnipresent as an object of critique, and rightly so – I hold that it is also worth revisiting the more black-and-white versions of 'us and Descartes'. And to do that, we need to go back to the seventeenth century, and to what Descartes first wrote.

This attempt to look anew at Cartesian philosophy is not just for the sake of defending historical accuracy, though I shall of course want to explain in clear terms what Descartes argued, and when, and how. That kind of historical and philosophical precision is just one feature within the broader horizon of an argument often made by early modernists: that looking to the past can still, even and especially in times of crisis, be a valuably defamiliarising process, allowing modernity to understand its own history and consider its own choices. There are real dangers involved in suggesting to our readers and our students that the seventeenth century stands for all that is bad and wrong, and that early modern thinkers are somehow less environmentally aware than we are. But even the wider goal – making a case for historicity, and the relevance of the history of ideas – is only one aspect of a more expansive critical landscape, which I would describe as follows. If we can reconsider Descartes, then we can add an extra level of precision to our objections, our ambitions, our future arguments, and our ecological attentiveness. Descartes is after all, and uncontroversially, one of the great philosophers of attentiveness. What does it mean to pay attention, and what should we pay attention to, and why? If we can come to more accurate terms with his philosophy, then we can also come to more accurate terms with our own imagined and projected alternatives.

This introduction to this Element will go into detail on the current picture in circulation, while also outlining an approach that I am calling *ecohistorical*. Early modern narratives about the world's ecosystems are rich and interesting and complex, and studying Descartes in context is helpful.

1.1 The Standard Account

The standard account is as follows: Descartes framed the world as essentially split between the realm of mind and that of inert matter. He is said to bring about 'the utter separation of mind from a mechanistic universe of matter which is most emphatically not a medium of thought or meaning, which is expressively dead' (Taylor 1989, 148). Because Descartes says clearly that humans are the only rational beings (i.e. on his account, the only ones possessed of a soul), this must mean that they are wholly separate from and superior to nature and non-human animals, who are considered mere mindless machines to be mastered and exploited at will. This is often seen as a kind of motivated reasoning: Descartes dismisses animal rationality precisely *in order to* abuse animals, as he subjugates the natural world to his own scientific ends. As Timothy Clark puts it:

> Inherited arguments, whether it be Aristotle on animals' lack of rationality or Descartes' preposterous claim of their lack of consciousness, come to seem no more than assertions made to justify a status quo in which animals are exploited solely as a resource for human beings. The issue takes an even more uncomfortable moral form in the context of a world that many see as entering the throes of a mass extinction event. (2019, 11)

And Jonathan Krell spells out the received causal connection between Descartes's thinking and the real and present crisis:

> We find ourselves in an environmental predicament in which nature – were it capable of acting like a human – would seem to be taking its revenge. Blizzards, hurricanes, and tornadoes are more severe than ever, both droughts and floods appear to be on the rise, poison ivy and bed–bugs are stronger and angrier than ever. For all this we can thank Descartes, among others. (2012, 3)

Descartes is therefore, on this account, the forefather of modern agro-industrial approaches to the natural world. He allows us to be extractive, brutal: 'To visit a modern Concentrated Animal Feeding Operation (CAFO) is to enter a world that for all its technological sophistication is still designed on seventeenth-century Cartesian principles: animals are treated as machines – "production units" – incapable of feeling pain' (Pollan 2006, 317). With Descartes, the status of non-human beings reaches its 'absolute nadir' (Singer 1975, 217). His thoughts on animals only scratch the surface of his (un)ethical account of nature in general: 'Descartes's ethic, just as much as his epistemology, calls for disengagement from world and body and the assumption of an instrumental stance towards them. It is of the essence of reason, both speculative and practical, that it push us to disengage' (Taylor 1989, 155). In simple terms, for Descartes, 'nothing non-intellectual really matters' (Midgley 1983, 11). His milieu or context – along with the very idea of nature, or environs, or ambience – is conceived as external to him and *therefore*, on this account, unimportant, to be processed, approved, or rejected by a heroic thinking mind endowed with the proper strength of will.

Even philosophers who disagree on ecocritical approaches agree that we need to abandon Descartes. In *The Natural Contract*, Michel Serres starts, as so many do, from part 6 of the *Discourse on Method*. Unlike the speculative philosophy of the scholastics, new scientific attitudes may make us 'as it were the masters and possessors of nature'.[1] Serres rejects the master words, 'mastery and possession',

> launched by Descartes at the dawn of the scientific and technological age, when our Western reason went off to conquer the universe. We dominate and appropriate it: such is the shared philosophy underlying industrial enterprise as well as so-called disinterested science, which are indistinguishable in this

[1] The reference is to part 6 of the *Discourse on Method*, in the standard edition by C. Adam and P. Tannery (Descartes 1996), vol. VI, p. 62. Subsequent references will appear in the text and footnotes using the abbreviation AT before the volume and page numbers. All translations from Descartes will follow, with occasional modifications, those of Cottingham et al., Gaukroger, Maclean, and Moriarty in Descartes 1985, 1991, 1998, 2006, 2008, and 2015, respectively. Other unattributed translations from French are my own.

> respect. Cartesian mastery brings science's objective violence into line, making it a well-controlled strategy. (Serres 1995, 32)

The contract of his title presupposes that nature should be granted a dignity symbiotic with, and equivalent to, the rights that the legal system has hitherto designated as 'human'. Luc Ferry counters Serres's form of 'deep ecology' with significant disdain, while still rejecting 'Cartesian anthropocentrism'. 'How', he asks, 'can we move beyond the antinomy of Cartesianism (which tends to deny creatures of nature any intrinsic value) and deep ecology (which considers the biosphere to be the only authentic subject of law)?' (1995, 140). The initial assumption of both critics – the first writing with an imaginative and poetic openness to other beings, the other espousing a more dismissive tone – is the same. The non-human world possesses zero value or interest for Descartes.

As a result of the dualisms that Descartes sets up or entrenches, so the story continues, deeply oppressive power structures have been allowed to form. These have spread across all aspects of our patriarchal society. The mind/body and subject/object dualisms bring along with them, via a number of 'linking postulates', not just dangerous human/animal and human/nature distinctions, but also male/female and reason/emotion divides (Plumwood 1993, 43). Thus, Descartes's name is often mentioned in pioneering ecofeminist accounts that highlight the many and – thanks to this body of work – now accepted ways in which women's oppression can correlate with the unjustified domination of 'mother' nature. 'Mother Nature was delivered to the laboratory to undergo scientific experimentation', writes Carolyn Merchant (1989 and 2010, 199), and women are correspondingly reduced to a body available for exploitation (labour, sex, reproduction) like any natural resource. As feminist environmental philosophy has developed along more intersectional lines, bringing in a wider variety of forms of oppression (racism, colonialism, classism . . .) and linking these compellingly and damningly to the degradation of the natural world, so Descartes has become associated by contamination with these modes of domination too, all intrinsically connected. As well as 'anthropocentric' and 'wrong', 'Cartesian' now often just means 'superior' and 'uncaring': the hegemony of reason is not just a dominant vision but 'a directing agency subordinating a functional domain' (Taylor 1989, 149). Thus, ecofeminist method displaces objectivity in favour of emotional intelligence – we should think about what we care about, and care about what we think (Warren 2000) – while 'Cartesian rationality separates science from ethics by excluding emotion from reason' (Glazebrook 2023, 4).

In response to the solidification of arrogant attitudes associated with Descartes (although often now without direct or primary reference to Descartes himself), a more recent and richly influential account proposes an alternative critical model, where *all* human agency is decentred and displaced. Such a model is elaborated notably across the career of Bruno Latour, a student of Michel Serres, and pursued by Jane Bennett in her account of 'vibrant matter' (Latour 1993, 2004, 2005; Bennett 2010). Bennett wants to unsettle 'the quarantines of matter and life' (2010, vii) and 'the onto-theological binaries of life/matter, human/animal' (2010, x). Agency and action need to be understood not as the inherent property of human beings as opposed to other beings, but as a nascent, evolving, dynamic feature of heterogeneous alliances that are hybrid and made up of both human and non-human participants. This gentle, non-anthropocentric politics is beautifully summed up in Latour's 'parliament of things' (1993, 142). The inanimate blends into the animate, for agency needs to be considered as shared by, because distributed across, *all* these participants. Human activity is inextricably entwined with the activity of the myriad other denizens of this earth, as well as with the activity of the earth itself. The ensuing task of finding an account of agency that is both ontologically distributed and powerfully decisive is all the more compelling and urgent (Crowley 2022).

1.2 Descartes, Differently

Occasionally, one does see Descartes's name employed differently in ecocritical literature, although such re-evaluations are scattered and non-systematic. Timothy Morton ventures 'the provocative, probably heretical and certainly, to many ecological ears, blasphemous, idea that Descartes, the whipping boy of ecological discourse, may have something to tell us about place' (Morton 2007, 176). Morton is interested in the sheer difficulty of overcoming subject–object dualism. The very idea of a 'kinship' with nature can be naively destructive, he holds, since human perception ends up revealing some form of non-identity with the natural world. It simply does; it cannot avoid it. This is because the 'I' that writes about being immersed in nature is still the 'I' that is writing about it: 'Even if "I" could be immersed in nature, and still exist as an *I*, there would remain the *I* who is telling you this, as opposed to the *I* who is immersed' (Morton 2007, 182). The 'dark ecology' that Morton recommends (2016) acknowledges and embraces that sense of difference – nature as inassimilable other – while also insisting that the self is formed by its environment, and that the ways we think are shared between us and other entities. Humans are intertwined with ecology in a Möbius strip, a strange loop in which two levels that appear separate twist into one another (Morton 2007, 177). 'Being ecological' includes a sense of 'my weird inclusion in what I'm experiencing' (Morton 2018, 202).

In the *Meditations*, Descartes's meditator knows very well that his doubts about the world are facilitated by the comforting ambient warmth of the fire next to him: 'I am here, sitting by the fire, wearing a dressing gown, holding this page in my hand', as the passage singled out by Morton (2007, 140) puts it. Only because he is comfortably ensconced can he allow a doubt to arise:

> How often my sleep at night has convinced me of all these familiar things – that I was here, wrapped in my gown, sitting by the fire – when in fact I was lying naked under the bedclothes! [. . .] When I think this over more carefully, I see plainly that there are never any sure signs by which being awake can be distinguished from being asleep [. . .]. (*First Meditation*, AT VII, 19)

And indeed, Morton has picked up on one of the most crucial moments in all of Cartesian philosophy. The fact that I think I am experiencing something in a particular way does not guarantee at all that I am in fact experiencing it. I cannot know that I am not now dreaming, and nor can you. And even if I *am* pretty sure that I am not dreaming right now, as I type these words (and so are you, as you read them), I can still level another doubt at that belief. Let's suppose that there is an evil genius, a deceiver of supreme power and cunning, who is deliberately and constantly deceiving me. But even in that case, counters the meditator, 'I too undoubtedly exist, if he is deceiving me; and let him deceive me as much as he can, he will never bring it about that I am nothing so long as I think I am something' (*Second Meditation*, AT VII, 25).

The radical doubt, and the radical *certainty* of the thinking that ensues in Meditation 2 (for doubting is a kind of thinking, so if *I* am doubting *I* cannot doubt that *I* am thinking, even if nothing else about the *world* or my *body* is true) – this is what gives us Cartesian dualism.[2] And yet that very dualism itself is sourced, as Morton notes, from the situatedness of the dressing gown and the fire, and from the fact that Descartes, in asking his readers to meditate themselves, is asking them to start from their own situatedness. (This is, after all, a pedagogical enterprise.) The engaging, sci-fi *strangeness* of these radical thought experiments is what seems to be most useful to Morton: Descartes is doing something like reintroducing 'the uncanny into the poetics of the home' (Morton 2007, 177). This is why Descartes 'does ecomimesis' (135), where ecomimesis is the rendering of one's environment, and '*strong* ecomimesis

[2] Descartes never called it that himself. *Le Robert* gives the first use of the term 'dualisme' in French as Pierre Bayle's *Dictionnaire historique et critique* (1697), à propos of the Manicheans. The German philosopher Christian Wolff applies it to Descartes's work in his *Psychologia rationalis* (1734). The OED has the first English usage in 1794, in T. J. Mathias's satirical poem *Pursuits of Literature*, where it is described as 'French jargon'.

purports to evoke the here and now of writing' (32). Descartes's version of ecomimesis does not collapse into nature, which is why Morton can embrace it. There is an honesty, Morton seems to be saying, in reflecting hard on one's own subject position, and nobody can accuse Descartes of not doing that. As Morton puts it, 'acknowledging the gap [in all forms of dualism] is a paradoxical way of having greater fidelity to things' (Morton 2007, 142); and, as he reiterates in conclusion, 'hanging out in the distance may be the surest way of relating to the nonhuman' (Morton 2007, 205).

Robert Macfarlane turns to another aspect of Descartes's work for a form of ecological encouragement: his thoughts, in *The Passions of the Soul*, on the kinds of attention generated by the passion of wonder. *The Passions of the Soul* (sometimes still neglected in Anglophone accounts of Descartes's work, which tend to focus on the *Discourse* and the *Meditations*) is written as an extension of a philosophical correspondence. In 1643, Descartes is quizzed, by Princess Elisabeth of Bohemia, on how the lived reality of mind–body union can coexist alongside the metaphysical distinction made in the *Meditations*.[3] If soul and body are distinct substances, how do we explain (a) voluntary movement (the action of the soul on the body) and (b) sensations and passions (the action of the body on the soul)? Descartes tries to explain; and in ordering and classifying the passions, he prioritises the experience of wonder, or wonderment, or awe. (This is a translation of the French 'admiration', which is something of a false friend in this context, since here it does not have the admiring moral connotations of the English.) The passion of wonder is a response to singularity or to novelty: to anything that exceeds the category of the familiar. Because a wondering response to an encounter happens before we have any knowledge of whether or not that encounter will be beneficial, it is defined by Descartes as 'the first passion of all' (art. 53, AT XI, 373). It brings with it an attentiveness associated with an urge to explain or give an account: 'In wonderment, the soul is suddenly taken by surprise, which causes it to consider attentively the objects that it finds rare and extraordinary' (art. 70, AT XI, 380). Wonder can contribute positively to enquiry, understanding, and the forming of long-term memories, writes Descartes (art. 75, AT XI, 384). This is what interests Macfarlane.

In his ongoing work on the vocabulary of the Anthropocene, Macfarlane has used Sianne Ngai's term 'stuplimity' (Ngai 2005) to signal wonder's opposite, a form of incapacity or 'outage' that can stem from continual exposure, no matter how horrifying, to the reality of environmental devastation: 'Like other unwholesome aspects of the Anthropocene, we mostly respond to mass

[3] The correspondence extends to Descartes's death in early 1650. For the initial query, see Elisabeth to Descartes, 6/16 May 1643, AT III, 661.

extinction with stuplimity: the aesthetic experience in which astonishment is united with boredom, such that we overload on anxiety to the point of outrage-outage' (Macfarlane 2016). And in an interview that pursues this interest in the language that we use to signal and to connect ourselves to human and more-than-human worlds, Macfarlane notes:

> Descartes says 'wonder is the first of all the passions', partly because he says it prompts us first to be astonished, and then to explain the source of that astonishment. I think that idea of amazement followed by the wish to understand how amazement is made is a very powerful two-stroke engine, as it were, for change. (Quoted in Hopkins 2018)

This emphasis on the productive capacity of Descartes's thinking about attention moves in the same area as Morton's. It is possible to say something useful about the particularity of human attentiveness, even as we see the highest goal of that attentiveness to be a recognition of our constitutive entanglement with the natural world.[4]

These critics open up a space for considering Descartes beyond the standard Anglophone absorption of his thinking. Looking at Descartes differently, in what follows, will also involve a corresponding attentiveness to what may be lost in translating him from French or Latin into English. As we have already seen, his position in the canon relies only on a proportion of his work: untranslatability has been a feature of the reception history. Much of Descartes's multi-volume, bilingual oeuvre is still somewhat obscure; dominant early modern forms such as familiar letters and scientific correspondence have not always been seen to translate into philosophy 'proper'; and some of the language used, from the term 'science' on, is inevitably multivalent, and untranslatable in that sense (Cassin 2014). As Stephanie Posthumus has suggested from within the discipline of French Studies, any project that highlights (un)translatability can be useful in promoting a diversity of attitudes and forms, and therefore, as the ecocritical imperative requires, countering the more homogenising forces of globalisation (Posthumus 2019, 607).

1.3 A Brute to the Brutes?

Of course, philosophical commentators have long countered some of the most frequent generalisations about Descartes's thinking. Most recently, Denis Kambouchner (2015 and 2023) has espoused a powerfully cliché-busting approach, bringing contemporary Cartesian scholarship to a wider audience,

[4] For the ecocritical rethinking of the modern legacy of romanticism, in which both Morton and Macfarlane play a part, see Goodbody in Westling 2013.

as in turn I hope to do here.[5] One piece in particular has been influential in the drawing up of this Element, which is conceived as an ecocritical extension of the argument in question. In 1978, *Philosophy* published an important article by John Cottingham on Descartes's treatment of animals. Titled 'A Brute to the Brutes?', it sought to counter the tendency, already standard in academic discourse, to lay at Descartes's door the disturbing belief that animals are not sentient beings. As Cottingham notes, to believe that a dog with a broken paw is not in pain when it whimpers would seem quite extraordinary, 'even for a philosopher' (Cottingham 1978, 551): that view is an exceptionally strong one and, Cottingham will argue, stronger than Descartes's own. Cottingham writes with a determination to revisit and properly explain the terms and structures of Descartes's mechanistic account of the world. The result is a careful elucidation of seven connected propositions:

(1) Animals are machines
(2) Animals are automata
(3) Animals do not think
(4) Animals have no language
(5) Animals have no self-consciousness
(6) Animals have no consciousness
(7) Animals are totally without feeling.

In the course of this enumeration, Cottingham notes, as Cartesian philosophers often do, that Descartes is not always as clear or distinct as he would like to be. We may nevertheless agree that Descartes holds propositions (1) through to (5). Descartes's main problem, as far as the reception of his thoughts on animals is concerned, stems from a confusion between proposition (5) and proposition (6): a slippage between *self-consciousness* and *consciousness*. The critical confusion lays Descartes open to the 'monstrous thesis' described in proposition (7), and Cottingham aims to explain and reduce these problems of interpretation.

In so doing, Cottingham engages throughout with Descartes's separation of body from mind. This dualism, as we have already seen, turns out not to be as strict as all that. Cottingham does not refer to the 1649 *Passions of the Soul*, the work in which (as prompted by Elisabeth of Bohemia) Descartes spends much more time on, and tries explicitly to explain, mind–body interaction. In a later article on 'Cartesian Trialism', he will add this emphasis (Cottingham 1985). However, he notes from the start that, even within the metaphysical protocol of

[5] Along with the succinct and humorous refutations in the work referenced, Kambouchner's recent Pléiade edition of the *Œuvres* (Descartes 2024a) will also contribute towards this rebalancing of opinion.

the *Meditations*, there is a fuzziness about dualism, in Meditation 6. We do not merely 'notice' that we are in pain, as a pilot observes that his ship is damaged, we notice it *while actually feeling it*; and this shows that there is a 'conjunctio et quasi permixtio' ('a union and so to speak a fusion') between mind and body (AT VII, 81; Cottingham 1978, 559). It is and has always been a problem for Cartesian philosophy that this intermingling is only briefly described, and not properly elucidated, in the *Meditations* themselves.

Because Descartes displays some 'fuzziness' (Cottingham 1978, 552, 558) about this psychophysiology, he is certainly vague on animal feelings too. However, there is no evidence that he held the view that animals are totally without feeling, and there is positive evidence to the contrary. The crucial point is that, for Descartes, human thinking equates to an extreme self-reflexivity: to think is to be aware, right now, of my own thinking. This means that 'I think, therefore I am' is a mistranslation of the 'je pense, donc je suis' of the *Discourse on Method*, often called 'the *cogito*' because of later Latin translations.[6] Philosophically speaking, the translation has to be 'I am thinking, therefore I am'. As Simon Blackburn puts it, 'Descartes's premise is not "I think" in the sense of "I ski", which can be true even if you are not at the moment skiing. It is supposed to be parallel to "I am skiing"' (1999, 19).

It follows that, in his *Principles of Philosophy*, Descartes defines thinking rather strongly and actively, as 'everything that takes place in us, while we are aware, *in so far as there is awareness of it in us*' (part 1, art. 9, AT VIII, 7). It can be helpful to consider that this focus on the *awareness of* our thinking finds a modern analogue in some kinds of cognitive behavioural therapy. Instead of thinking, for instance, 'this is hopeless' or 'I mess everything up', this kind of therapy encourages us to add, 'I notice that I am having the thought that this is hopeless' and 'I notice that I am having the thought that I mess everything up'. The therapy creates a powerful distance between the content and the form of the thinking. The content, considered by itself, has no determining truth value. For Descartes, when I think I see an object, the existence of that object can be put in doubt. What can't be doubted is my awareness that *I think I see an object*. (In the end, the existence of an external physical world, like the rejection of the idea of the evil genius, can be confirmed only via belief in God: being infinitely perfect, God would not systematically deceive us.)

The reflexive self-consciousness outlined here is what animals do not possess, according to Descartes. It relies for him on a soul defined by its rationality, which again animals do not possess. That animals are denied rationality is not a surprising point for Descartes to make, being an orthodox position at this time,

[6] The Latin *Meditations* do not themselves contain the phrase *cogito, ergo sum*.

found for example in Augustine and Aquinas.[7] However, Descartes is more trenchant than previous thinkers on the nature of the soul: the role of the soul is to think, and not to animate a living body. Crucially, however, some kinds of awareness (e.g. sensation or instinct) *do not require* this reflexive thinking; and we shall discuss this in more detail in a moment, when we look at the mechanics of Cartesian bodies. This feature of Descartes's thought is what tends to go unnoticed or misunderstood by his critics. This is why we see the sorts of comments in some of the ecocritical literature cited in Section 1.1, given significant impetus since Cottingham by works such as *Descartes's Error: Emotion, Reason and the Human Brain* (Damasio 1994) and *Straw Dogs: Thoughts on Humans and Other Animals* (Gray 2002). This is before we get onto popular psychology (sample headline: 'Damn you and your Dumb Dualism, Descartes').[8] When Gray (2002, 59) writes, for example, 'It has been an axiom since Descartes that knowledge presupposes conscious awareness. But sensation and perception do not depend on consciousness, still less on self-awareness', he is making a point, supposedly *against* Descartes, that Descartes himself made. As Descartes puts it: 'The body can be moved to take flight by the mere lay-out of its organs with no input from the soul' (*Passions of the Soul*, art. 38, AT XI, 358).

So, Cottingham's conclusions, though highly influential and often cited in Descartes studies, seem not to have embedded themselves in the wider humanities. Perhaps his article on the animals is remembered more for its assertion that Descartes certainly agreed with propositions (1)–(5), revolving around mechanism and automation, than for his rejection of proposition (7). These points can sound quite monstrous enough by themselves, to modern ears. Indeed, Cottingham's careful discussion of what propositions (1)–(5) actually mean, in context and according to early modern ways of thinking, has not made it into standard academic discourse either.

1.4 An Ecohistorical Approach

In the present Element, I aim to extend Cottingham's careful critique of Descartes on animals to a study of Descartes and the non-human world in general, and thereby to update his arguments for the current ecocritical environment. I hold

7 Later medieval thinkers tended to amalgamate two sets of views: Aristotle's statement that animals had nutritive and sensitive, and not rational, souls, and the biblical doctrines found in Gen.1, 26–28, on man alone being made in the image of God (Oelze 2018).

8 This is 'an open letter to Rene Descartes about the importance of holistic health'. www.psychologytoday.com/gb/blog/black-belt-brain/202101/damn-you-and-your-dumb-dualism-descartes. In general, the blogosphere and social media should not be trusted as a source of information about Descartes's work.

that one way to move towards achieving the crucial goals of the environmental humanities – including a proper consideration of crisis, such that we pose the very real question of whether we can continue to inhabit the earth – is to show that these goals have always been crucial. In other words, one way to increase the political effectiveness of distributed accounts of agency, such that we can counter the heedless destruction of other human and non-human entities around us, is to understand very clearly that an extractive ambition *cannot be justified* – and even in the texts by Descartes that are so often given as its source.

Descartes's own ambitions for the future include his most infamous line of all: the hope expressed in the *Discourse on Method* that we should one day become 'as it were the masters and possessors of nature' (AT VI, 62), sometimes also given as 'the lords and masters of nature'. This goal, though, is set precariously against a backdrop of his present reality, which brings various kinds of impossibility with it. Because this particular formulation is forbiddingly alien and off-putting, it is easy to want to brush over or gloss it. Even so, it is worth reading on and around. When we do, we see that, like so much early modern literature, it contains and presupposes and works from an acknowledgement of human *inadequacy*: human exceptionalism in a *bad* sense. Everywhere around it we see our capacity to fail, to fall, our downfall: this is what the ambition is set against. Above all, we see (in the very next sentence) the fact of our physical vulnerability, the sheer difficulty of 'the preservation of health, which is without doubt the highest good and the foundation of all other goods in this life' (AT VI, 62). And with this very present fragility comes a set of emphases and priorities that we often neglect, to our detriment.

To read, observe, and listen to what is left of the seventeenth century is to experience, daily, the coexistence of bodies and their landscape: ashes to ashes, dust to dust. It is to be forced to think about a time before and beyond the human, because human lifespans are at this time vanishingly short and precarious, and traumatic bereavement is a shared norm. Even by the mid eighteenth century, when statistics began to be gathered more systematically, half of all children died before the age of ten, and life expectancy stood at twenty-five years.[9] Few adults could have made it to adulthood without seeing a dead body. Descartes's own lifetime (1596–1650) was marked by climatic instability and vicious cold;[10] by the horrors of geopolitical warfare in the form of the Thirty Years War (1618–1648); and by the local shocks and after-shocks of recurrent civil

9 www.ined.fr/fr/tout-savoir-population/graphiques-cartes/graphiques-interpretes/esperance-vie-france/

10 These phenomena are associated with heightened global volcanic activity globally. See Stoffel et al. 2022, which investigates the sources of the eruptions of the 1630s and 1640s and their possible impact on contemporary climate using ice core, tree-ring, and historical evidence. In the

wars, all of which brought persistent epidemics and harvest crises and unusually high infant mortality.[11] Estimates of military and civilian deaths in the Thirty Years War, for example, range from 4.5 to 12 million, of which only a minor number died in the fighting. War-related food shortages and outbreaks of epidemic disease – typhus, typhoid, dysentery, influenza, and plague – were by far the greatest killers (Parker 1987, 211). Descartes and his contemporaries lived through various and repeated waves of plague (bubonic, pneumonic, septicaemic) with, in some European cities, mortality rates of 60 per cent and more (Alfani 2013, 417).[12] His biography tells a not remotely unusual story: he lost his mother as an infant, and his daughter, Francine, to scarlet fever when she was five.[13]

The work of the ecohistorian comes up against the harshness of this world: its complex pressures, movements, currents, shifts, and slides, as it tries and fails to document the lived experience of precarity. 'In what annals has it ever been read', asks Petrarch in 1348,

> that houses were left vacant, cities deserted, the country neglected, the fields too small for the dead and a fearful and universal solitude over the whole earth? Oh happy people of the future, who have not known these miseries, and perchance will class our testimony with the fables! (Petrarch in Deaux 1969, 94).

Three centuries later, both testimonies and fables, including the *Discourse on Method* – 'I am putting this essay forward only as an historical record, or if you prefer, a fable' (AT VI, 4) – were still set against the backdrop of a material reality shot through with displacement and disease. John Donne knew it in London in 1626: the thick atmosphere of death, the 'lamentable calamity' in which 'the dead were buried, and thrown up again before they were resolved into dust, to make room for more' (1919, 61). Because Donne is living through it, he gives us a horrific literalisation of our imbrication with the elements:

Northern Hemisphere as a whole, '1641 was the third-coldest summer recorded over the past six centuries, 1643 was the tenth-coldest, and 1642 was the twenty-eighth coldest – three landmark winters in a row' (Parker 2008, 1068). On these 'hyper' moments of the 'little ice age', see in particular Ladurie 2004. On the co-occurrence of the coolest part of the Little Ice Age (1594–1677) with the reforestation that followed the European genocide of Indigenous Americans, and the move to name the Anthropocene accordingly, see Lewis and Maslan 2015.

11 Even among historians who reject the narrative of a 'general crisis', it is generally accepted that 'seventeenth-century Europe was more beset by demographic and economic difficulties, internal social turbulence, and major wars than either the sixteenth or the eighteenth' (Bergin 2001, 3).

12 The bubonic plague or Black Death, caused by the bacterium *Yersinia pestis*, is said to have killed at least 30 per cent of populations across Europe and along its path from South Asia to the Middle East. Not even the worst-case scenarios of epidemiologists during the recent Covid-19 pandemic envisaged anything like such a loss (Glatter and Finkelman 2020).

13 Descartes never married, but acknowledged the paternity of Francine and remained in touch with her mother throughout her life. For the legend that Descartes constructed a life-size automaton representing her, see Kang 2017 and Section 2.4.

'Every puff of wind within these walls, may blow the father into the son's eye, or the wife into her husband's, or his into hers, or both into their children's, or their children's into both' (1919, 61). In France, the abbess Angélique Arnauld also knew this terrifying here and now, her vast correspondence (1620–1661) studded with illness and suffering, 'trembling' in 1653 at the thought of the return of the civil war that had been ravaging France since 1648: 'almost all the men gone, only orphaned children left' (Arnauld 2020, 29 January 1653, 1119). How can we possibly cultivate our land, she asks, with 'a third of the world dead' (28 January 1654, 1294)?

Descartes, in his own philosophically engaged way, and even from the geographical isolation that he sought all his life, wrote about this reality too. He knew the need to explain human suffering as a function of God's will, and the salutary rescaling that this brings with it, such that we 'come to terms with the vast idea of the extent of the universe' (this is also the most important of all his scientific commitments, as we shall see), and therefore *condemn*, scientifically speaking, the idea that 'the heavens were created only for the service of the earth, and the earth only for man' (letter to Elisabeth, 15 September 1645, AT IV, 292). Descartes's own ambitions, correctly described by his early reader Blaise Pascal, are 'eye-popping' (Pascal 1962, fragment 199). But beyond the realm of the immortal soul there are always limits, and Descartes himself outlines the 'presumptuous arrogance' that lies in wanting 'to take a share in God's counsels' (to Elisabeth, 15 September 1645, AT IV, 292). This false devotion – thinking ourselves close to God – leads, in a climactic moment of the 1649 *Passions of the Soul*, to 'the greatest crimes that human beings can commit: such as betraying cities, assassinating rulers, and exterminating whole peoples, for the simple reason that they do not follow one's own opinions' (art. 190, AT XI, 472). Descartes chooses these examples for a reason: they are all around.[14] The world is unhinged and raw.

[14] For this crisis in its global dimension, see Parker 2008, 1053, which gives a useful summary in introduction: 'The mid-seventeenth century saw more cases of simultaneous state breakdown around the globe than any previous or subsequent age: something historians have called "The General Crisis." In the 1640s, Ming China, the most populous state in the world, collapsed; the Polish-Lithuanian Commonwealth, the largest state in Europe, disintegrated; much of the Spanish monarchy, the first global empire in history, seceded; and the entire Stuart monarchy rebelled – Scotland, Ireland, England, and its American colonies. In addition, just in the year 1648, a tide of urban rebellions began in Russia (the largest state in the world), and the Fronde Revolt paralyzed France (the most populous state in Europe); meanwhile, in Istanbul (Europe's largest city), irate subjects strangled Sultan Ibrahim, and in London, King Charles I went on trial for war crimes (the first head of state to do so). In the 1650s, Sweden and Denmark came close to revolution; Scotland and Ireland disappeared as autonomous states; the Dutch Republic radically changed its form of government; and the Mughal Empire, then the richest state in the world, experienced two years of civil war following the arrest, deposition, and imprisonment of its ruler'.

The ecohistorical approach that I am advocating tries to think its way into early modern knowledge changes in context, via local understandings of life and death, animality and mechanism, history and futurity, rationality and passion. In this way, ecohistoricism takes concepts that are crucial to the environmental humanities and shows that they have a history, and need to be studied historically. In what follows, I shall elaborate upon these introductory comments by examining the following seven propositions, each exemplifying a thesis that is often associated with Descartes's work. In so doing, I echo Cottingham's structure, while expanding on his points from an ecocritical angle.

(1) Descartes's mechanistic universe is automated and lifeless.
(2) Humans are entirely distinct from the non-human world.
(3) The *ego cogitans* at the centre of everything.
(4) We can subjugate animals as we wish.
(5) We can master and possess nature as a whole.
(6) Human action can and should be performed with total rational control.
(7) The soul's only function is to think.

Turning over and problematising each proposition in turn, I shall hold that Descartes rejects propositions (1)–(6). Thesis (7) is the only one that Descartes holds in any unambiguous sense; and even then, it needs to be set in context.

2 Seven Propositions

2.1 Descartes's Mechanistic Universe Is Automated and Lifeless

Matter, in Descartes, is part of a mechanical system: the material world can be conceived of as the working of an immense machine. Matter is extended (there is no unfilled space), and, despite appearances, all bodies and the space around them are composed of this same extended matter. Thus, there is no real difference between space and corporeal substance. This differentiates Descartes from Aristotle, for whom four distinct qualities combine to form the four elements: earth, air, fire, and water. For Descartes, matter is inert and passive, but *only* in the sense, later emphasised by Newton, of *remaining in whatever state it is in at a given time*, and *not changing its state spontaneously* (see *Principles*, part 2, art. 37). Bodies are constantly interacting in the Cartesian system. Descartes thinks, for example, that 'by simply walking, a man makes the entire mass of the earth move ever so slightly, since he is putting his weight now on one spot, now on another' (letter to Mersenne, December 1638, AT II, 467).

This mechanistic account relies on God's mysterious purpose in creating the world in the first place. God is the primary cause of all things and their motion, and always conserves the same quantity of motion in the universe. So, the same amounts of 'motion and rest' are conserved in the universe as a whole, distributed differently in different parts of the universe at different times, as a consequence of the way that God is immutable. Individual bodies are 'parts of matter' and their boundaries are determined by their motion relative to their immediate neighbours. Matter is infinitely divisible, to the point of being imperceptibly and unimaginably small. In sum: all matter possesses size, shape, position, and motion, and its functionality can be explained by the interaction of these properties. Its every aspect requires scientific description and is available to analysis.[15]

The broad mechanistic outlines of this philosophy place Descartes in line with his contemporaries, from Francis Bacon to Galileo Galilei, Thomas Hobbes, Pierre Gassendi, and Walter Charleton. It would, however, be a mistake to infer from this that machines and mechanisms are for Descartes just a pile of parts: technically interesting, but cold, inactive, dully homogeneous, and to be set to utilitarian ends. Affective reactions to mechanism have changed over time. Jessica Riskin (2016) has shown powerfully that, to understand early modern intellectual history, we need to think our way into an entirely different way of conceiving machines. We need to associate mechanism with various potent semantic fields that now seem unfamiliar to us, acculturated as we are to industrial scales of mechanical production. As she beautifully puts it, these may be 'forceful, restless, purposeful, sentient, perceptive' (2016, 6): certainly not lifeless or dead. Riskin shows the prevalence, well into the seventeenth century and alongside 'the scientific revolution', of a persisting ancient and medieval tradition 'in which matter and mechanism remained active and vital, and in which automata represented spirit in every corporeal guise available and life at its very liveliest' (2016, 43).[16]

Descartes writes explicitly that the difference between artificial bodies and natural bodies is not salient to him. Importantly: this means less that *natural bodies are to be considered artificial* than that *artificial bodies are considered to be natural*. He is trying to concentrate on the means by which *any*

[15] These two paragraphs are a summary of some of the main points made in the second part of the 1644 *Principia* (*Principles of Philosophy*), translated into French in 1647 (AT VIII, 40–80; AT IX.2, 63–102). These points also reprise his work in *The World*, written early in his career but only published posthumously. The publications in *The World* are suppressed 'simply to obey the church' (letter to Mersenne, February 1634, AT 1, 281), on account of the controversy surrounding Galileo and the Copernican belief that the earth moves around the sun. For a more detailed account of Descartes's natural philosophy, see Gaukroger 2002.

[16] Historians of early modern science like regularly to point out the artificiality of the 'scientific revolution' label, as in the first sentence of Steven Shapin's textbook on the topic: 'There was no such thing as the Scientific Revolution, and this is a book about it' (Shapin 1996, 1). For a more up-to-date treatment of this terminology and its history, see Secord 2023.

movement in the world, visible or perceptible or otherwise, human or non-human, is produced and explained. Thus, in the concluding section of the *Principles*, he does not 'recognize any difference between artefacts and natural bodies except that the operations of artefacts are for the most part performed by mechanisms large enough to be easily perceivable by the senses', where effects produced by natural means 'almost always depend on structures so minute that they completely elude our senses'. And he clarifies in the same passage that, 'All the rules of mechanics also belong to physics, in such a way that all artificial things are also natural' (*Principles*, part 4, no. 203, AT VIII, 325–326).

The main explanatory analogy here, as very often in Descartes, is with machines in the form of clocks or watches: 'So, for example, when a clock tells the time by means of the wheels of which it is made, that is no less natural to it than it is to a tree to produce fruit' (*Principles*, part 4, art. 203, AT VIII, 326). Similarly, in the *Treatise on Man* (part of *The World*, along with the *Treatise on Light*), the bodily functions follow 'in this machine simply from the disposition of the organs as wholly naturally as the movements of a clock or other automaton follow from the disposition of its counterweights or wheels' (AT XI, 202). After several pages on the movement of the heart and the arteries in the *Discourse on Method*, Descartes concludes that the entire discussion follows necessarily from the disposition of organs that one can see, from the heat that one can feel, and from the nature of blood that one can know from observation – again just as the movement of a clock follows from the force, position, and shape of its mechanical components (AT VI, 50). And in the *Passions of the Soul*, the difference between a living and dead body is the same as the difference between a functional and a broken watch (art. 6, AT XI, 331).

Given the prominence of the clock-machine in Descartes's discussion of human and non-human nature, it is worth getting to grips with what a clock really *is* in the seventeenth century. The earliest mechanical clocks used a system of pulleys and weights to coordinate a striking movement, but the invention of the spring mechanism in the fifteenth century changed clock-making entirely. By the time Descartes starts writing, a clock can range from delightfully small – pocket watches, tabletop clocks, mantel clocks – to awe-inspiringly large, all these featuring in the most renowned paintings of the age (see Faraday 2019). Either way, the fact of its mechanism makes it impressively beautiful, and wondrously intricate, if also breakable. A clock is not necessarily entirely utilitarian, nor even straightforwardly precise: 'Until the mid-seventeenth century the clock remained an inaccurate timekeeper' (Bedini 1980, 21). Before Christiaan Huygens patented the pendulum clock in 1657, after Descartes's death, clocks were accurate to around fifteen minutes per day at best.[17] Sundials ('horloges au soleil', or 'sun-clocks' in French) remained the most popular time-telling device long after the clock's accuracy improved (Bedini 1980, 22; Landes 1983, 121–122; Faraday 2019, 241).[18]

Our notion that machines (including clocks) work 'like clockwork' – in perfectly regular, fatalistic, lifelessly automated ways – is therefore an anachronism in this context, for all the weight it has in modern accounts of Descartes. In English, the earliest use of 'clockwork' as denoting regularity and precision, and 'without life or sense', is given in the Oxford English Dictionary as 1679, in John Goodman's *Penitent Pardon'd.* (Other uses make clockwork like lacework, or woodwork: 'work with clocks'.) Descartes on machines, in the first half of the seventeenth century, is closer to those older accounts that make *automaton* describe a thing constructed by mechanics so as to seem to work with miraculous spontaneity, *self-moving* because without any visible cause. 'I scarcely believed my eyes, though I watched it every day', writes Angelo Poliziano in 1494 when describing the astronomical clock, or *machinula automata*, of the great artisan Lorenzo della Volpaia (Poliziano 2006, 273; see also Wilson-Lee 2025, 79). Thanks to the intrinsic wonder of this 'little machine' as it models the movements of the planets and predicted the timings of full moons, sunrises, sunsets, and even solar and lunar eclipses, the transfixed Poliziano is also transported back in time, to the age of Archimedes: 'Back when I read that Archimedes of Syracuse had once constructed something of this kind, my belief, even in the case of such a master, wavered – belief which this man of ours [Lorenzo] has now freed from doubt' (2006, 274). One of many legends about Archimedes's astonishing skill suggested that he had used the metal magnetite to draw nails out of and sink the ships of Greek enemies; this legend in turn encouraged the ancient idea that magnets, acting mechanically and at a distance, are both lively and ensouled. Aristotle attributes this view to Thales of Miletus, in the course of his own reconfiguring of the animate soul as nutritive, sensitive, and rational, in plants, animals, and humans, respectively (*De Anima* 1.2, 405a19-21).

For Descartes, rejecting Aristotle in turn, the soul is only rational, and is the distinguishing mark of the thinking being (= the human being), not the

[17] Christiaan Huygens was the son of Descartes's friend Constantijn, who is now best known as a poet but was in the 1630s deeply engaged in a correspondence with Descartes about the science of optical lenses.

[18] See also, in the English context, Faraday's summary of Thomas Scot's anti-Catholic satire 'Solarium', which describes a disagreement between a church clock and a sundial. The sundial represents the unassailable truth of Scripture, punning on the 'Sonne [/sun] of Righteousness', and the clock stands for the machinations of the Church, which has fallen out of step with the dial over the centuries and is now inaccurate. Thomas Scot, *Philomythie* (1622) in Faraday 2019, 247 (note 38).

animate being. It is never a support for the organic functions of life. Even so, Descartes is not always so very far from the lively work of the Renaissance humanists and their reception of classical texts.[19] Many liked to advertise the immense imaginative, creative power of human ingenuity, transporting us forward into an agreeable future as well as back to the Ancients. For Lorenzo Valla (1406–1457), a massive tower clock of the kind seen in Italian cities

> has, so to speak, a life of its own, as it moves spontaneously, and makes the days and nights for man. Not only does it reveal the time to the eye, but it also announces it to the ears of those far away and at home, as the bell which is placed on top specifies the number. Nothing could be more useful or pleasant than this. (Valla, *Gesta Ferdinandi*, 194, quoted in Grafton 2023, 51)

Combining utility and pleasure, Valla is echoing Horace's *Art of Poetry*, and the extent of human power over nature relies on a fabulous mix of artistic and technical skills. This intermingling of art and science, such that there is in fact a very fine line between magus and engineer, was very familiar. Roger Bacon (c. 1214–1292) had advocated a practical alchemy that also promised a futuristic power: teaching 'how to make noble metals and pigments, and many other things, better and more plentifully by artificial means than nature herself makes them'; and, in the long run, contributing to the overall alchemical goal of extending human life (Bacon 1859, 40).

Bacon is perhaps known above all for the legends of his own automaton, the talking head.[20] In his account, his *scientia experimentalis* could facilitate achievements that outdid magic, while still engendering a world of marvels:

> Instruments of navigation can be made without men to row, so that very great ships, in river and ocean alike, are moved by the power of one man, and faster than if they had a full crew. Similarly, carriages can be made that move without animals, with an incredible force, like, I suspect, that of the scythed chariots with which the ancients fought. Likewise, instruments of flight can be made, so that a man sits in the middle of the instrument, turning a device, which makes artificially constructed wings beat the air, in the manner of a flying bird. (Bacon, *Epistola de secretis operibus artis et naturae*, 532–533, quoted in Grafton 59)

[19] On the long and complex histories of the word 'humanism' from an ecocritical perspective (the *anthropos* vs. the *homo*), see Usher 2016.

[20] This we see in the anonymous sixteenth-century prose romance *The Famous History of Friar Bacon,* and the c. 1592 play by Robert Greene, *The Honourable History of Friar Bacon and Friar Bungay*, in which Bacon uses diabolical magic and 'necromantic charms' to get a brass head to speak (see Greene 1958; and, in the context of a larger group of legends about speaking heads, Kang 2011).

In this way, 'magic was not only unlawful but unnecessary: devices crafted by human intellect and energy could produce wonder' (Grafton 2023, 59). These accounts are shot through with the liveliness of experience as confirming and applying the laws of nature: the new engineers are the new Archimedes, their inventions or 'ingenia' unevenly straddling magic and mathematics, harking back to the lively magnets of the Ancients even as their mechanics are explored, explained, and illustrated in the most detailed technical terms.

The obsession with liveliness persists in Descartes's philosophy, as it does in the work of his contemporaries. His correspondent Kenelm Digby describes the great royal mint in Segovia in Spain as possessing a marvellous dynamism, with engines and stamps and presses and pumps moving together in such active unison that

> we call the entire thing *Automatum*, or *se movens*, or a living creature. Which also may be fittly compared to a joyner, or a painter, or other craftsman, that had his tooles so exactly fitted about him, as when he had occasion to do any thing in his trade, his toole for that action were already in the fittest position for it, to be made use of [. . .]. (Digby 1644, 208)

An equivalent wonder in the seventeenth century was the cathedral clock in Strasbourg, which Descartes mentions, and which took vivacity to extremes (see Riskin 2016, 18, for an illustration). One highlight was a moving cockerel that could crow at noon; this is a variant on a common feature, the figure of a man striking out the hour known as Jacquemart, or 'Jack-o-the-clock'. Uncommonly, though, the rooster was accompanied in this case by (among others) the Magi, virgin, and child; a selection of Roman Gods; an angel; babies, boys, and men of various ages; a mechanical Christ; and a personification of death, all against a backdrop of carillon music, a setting to a Pater Noster. These machines represent an astonishing moving spectacle. (That a talking head could be made to pronounce all the words in a Pater Noster, as in the legends just mentioned, is by contrast dismissed by Descartes as 'imposture' (AT 1, 25).)

Descartes's biographer Baillet suggests that he lived in Saint-Germain around 1615–1616, in which case he would have been able to gain first-hand knowledge of the marvellous automata found in the Royal Gardens and described in his *Treatise on Man*; he also probably knew the 1615 treatise of the garden architect and engineer Salomon de Caus.[21] He writes in the course of his *Treatise on Man* of 'artificial fountains, mills, and other similar machines

[21] De Caus designed and produced automata for the Garden of the Palatinate at Heidelberg for Elisabeth Stuart (wife of Frederick V, later King of Bohemia; their daughter, Princess Elisabeth, is the correspondent of Descartes). De Caus dedicated Book II of his 1615 *Les Raisons des forces mouvantes* to her, explicating the hydraulic principles on which fountain automata were based.

which, even though they are only made by men, have the power to move of their own accord in various ways' (AT 11, 120). Indeed, Descartes may plausibly have devised and constructed automata himself; this notion was introduced in 1670 by one of his editors, Nicolas-Joseph Poisson.[22] What is certain is that the points made about all such human-made automata, which can be analysed and explained in all their wonder, extend far beyond themselves by analogy: 'And, as I am supposing that this machine [the human body] is made by God, I think you will agree that it is capable of a greater variety of movements than I could possibly imagine in it, and that it exhibits a greater ingenuity than I could possibly ascribe to it' (AT XI, 120).

Just like these wondrous machines, but on a vastly more ingenious scale, bodies made by God avail themselves of the hydraulic movements of air and fluid. It makes sense that musical organs are another key machine for Descartes – and he appeals directly in the *Treatise on Man* to those who might have 'had the curiosity to look at the organs in our churches' (AT XI, 165). (Many churches, including Strasbourg, had extraordinarily intricate automata attached to their organs as well as to their clocks.) We can think of our own bodily organs, our heart or our arteries, 'as being like the bellows of an organ, which push air into the wind chests; and of external objects, which displace certain nerves, causing spirits from the brain cavities to enter certain pores, as being like the fingers of the organist, which press certain keys and cause the wind to pass from the wind chests into certain pipes' (AT XI, 165). Human-made automata sound and move simultaneously; divine-made automata (i.e. bodies) do the same, but in exponentially more sophisticated ways.

Matter works mechanically, for Descartes, but that does not mean that it is inert in the sense of 'unresponsive or dull', passive in the sense of 'devoid of liveliness', or everywhere the same. Descartes's mechanistic universe is indeed 'at its most authentically mechanical when discussing life' (Dear 1998, 59). The machines of the world, as they function in the first half of the seventeenth century, are fragile, beautiful, reactive, mobile, and wonderfully complex. Descartes's world shares these properties.

2.2 Humans Are Entirely Distinct from the Non-Human World

As we have seen, all natural phenomena can be explained on the basis of the interaction between matter and movement, and all bodies are made up of particles that can be too small to be perceived (so the functional is not always

[22] In his *Commentaire ou remarques sur la Méthode de René Descartes*, Nicolas-Joseph Poisson claims to have read in the philosopher's writings of how he made various automata, including a magnet-operated figure of a man on a tightrope, a flying pigeon, and a pheasant chased by a spaniel (Poisson 1670, 156).

visible). In the *Discourse*, Descartes recaps his thoughts on all bodies in the context of the wider animal kingdom, considering the bones, muscles, nerves, arteries, veins, and all the other parts that are in the body of every animal, and detailing how this all works 'comme une machine' – not just '*like* a machine' but '*as* a machine' (part 5; AT VI, 56).

This work sets up a radical *continuity* between human and animal bodies, which all function in exactly the same way. God has made *all* bodies as though forming a statue or a machine made of earth, and has done so 'tout exprès', quite deliberately, so as to give them not only the desired outward appearance but also the intricate inward disposition that allows them to function (AT XI, 120). All the basic functions of life and sentience are common to human and non-human animals:

> All the movements that we make without our will contributing to them (as happens often when we breathe, walk, eat, and do all the actions that we have in common with animals) depend only on the formation of our parts and on the course that the spirits, excited by the heat of the heart, naturally follow in the brain, the nerves and the muscles

– and here again Descartes has recourse to the analogy of a watch – 'in the same way that the movement of a watch is produced by the sole force of its spring and the configuration of its wheels' (*Passions of the Soul*, art. 16, AT XI, 341–342).

It can be helpful also to emphasise the limits of the correspondence between bodies (divine-made) and machines (human-made). God made our bodies work in the same way as a watch – they are part of God's mechanistic universe, so they *are* machines – and we have seen what this means. But there is some level of disanalogy too, because to say that all bodies function as machines is not the same thing as saying that all machines function as bodies. Machines and automata, along with human and animal bodies, can have various beautiful, intricate, lively, and responsive properties, and this is important for our understanding of Descartes's thought; but we can say this without holding that clocks possess lively and receptive functions in precisely the same way as animals. There has to be some differentiation in the universe: animals may be a machine, but this particular kind of machine is so extraordinarily complex, so 'astounding' (AT VI, 56), that it can be manufactured only by God. God's machines will always be 'incomparably more complex' than anything that we could come up with (to Mersenne, March 1638, AT 2, 41).

Thus, animals, both human and non-human, have all sorts of fascinating instincts and forms of feeling. If their foot is placed too close to a fire, they will move it away. If they are confronted by a threat, they will try to protect themselves, or turn and escape. Non-human animals, indeed, excel at these instinctive responses. They are similar to human animals in this respect, but sometimes superior: as Descartes says, 'some of them are stronger than us, and I believe that there may also be some animals which have a natural intelligence capable of deceiving the shrewdest human beings' (Letter to Newcastle, 23 November 1646, AT IV, 573). In this same letter, Descartes credits animals with some kinds of bodily passion, such as hope or fear; they can communicate such passions to each other and to us, although such passions are not 'passions of the soul' and do not count as thought in that sense. Their 'shrewdness' is not what Descartes calls a rational intelligence, but it is no less striking for that. If there is a gap between human and animal here, it is detrimental to the human.

Both the recoil from the fire and the escape from the predator are behavioural phenomena that rely, crucially for Descartes, on the 'course of the spirits' just mentioned (*Passions of the Soul*, art. 16, AT XI, 341–342). These are 'animal spirits', which are also described in great detail in the *Treatise on Man* and in the correspondence. They are the swiftest, smallest, most refined, and most volatile components of the blood, which are transported rapidly around the body. (Like his contemporaries, Descartes has a profound interest in how blood moves around the body: he famously disagreed with Harvey, saying that the circulation of blood is due to expansion and contraction resulting from the production of heat in the heart, and not due to any pumping action (AT XI, 241–245). This was swiftly refuted.) In Cartesian philosophy, animal spirits are the basis of all animal functioning, up to and including the brain's task of receiving sensations from the world or (in the case of human animals only) taking instructions from the soul. Animal spirits can even, despite the name, explain plant functioning, since Descartes follows an understanding that the circulation of sap in plants works in the same way as the circulation of blood around bodies: both movements are judged to be caused by heat, and it is not at all surprising to Descartes when he is shown a plant (*l'herbe sensitive*) whose leaves automatically close when touched (to Mersenne, 16 October et 13 November 1639, AT II 595 et 619; see Gaukroger 2002, 187).

Descartes's explanation for all basic physiology relies on a kind of 'subtle matter', the smallest category of extended matter, found everywhere in the material universe and forming a vast continuum across it. He holds that

> the only difference between this subtle matter and terrestrial bodies is that it is made up of much smaller particles which do not stick together and are always in very rapid motion. And because of this, when they pass through the gaps in terrestrial bodies and impinge on the particles of which the bodies are made up, they often make them vibrate, or even dislodge them and sweep some of them away. (Letter to Vorstius, 19 June 1643, AT III, 687)

The terrestrial particles that are swept away by subtle matter in this fashion make up *air*, *spirits*, and *flame*, where the spirit particles are more agitated than those that make up the air alone, but less agitated than those that make up flame.

Turning to animals whose heat is produced in the liver and heart, Descartes goes into more detail on how a progressive process of rarefaction transforms these spirits from 'natural spirits' into 'vital spirits' (this happens as food passes from the stomach into the veins), and then from 'vital spirits' into 'animal spirits' (to Vorstius, 19 June 1643, AT I, 687–688). During this process, these particles become so small, subtle, and quick that they have the power to reach the brain, where they are filtered by the pineal gland. From there they flow through to the nerves, where they are able to dictate the movement of the muscles to which each nerve belongs. So, the pineal gland is the foremost mediator between the senses and the motor nerves in animals; in humans, the pineal gland is also the seat of the soul (*Passions of the Soul*, art. 35, AT XI, 354). (Descartes supposes that this must be the case because the gland is the only part of the brain that is not divided into symmetrical halves. Therefore, he says, it must be responsible for uniting the images from the two eyes and senses from the two halves of the body, and transmitting them onwards to the mind. Along with his thoughts on the circulation of the blood, Descartes's depiction of the pineal gland is another aspect of his scientific work that was dismissed in his lifetime.) In all animals, the pineal gland can represent an image and form a cognitive stimulus. This goes beyond the reflex action that is also common to plants, which relies only on a circulatory system (Gaukroger 2002, 190).

Far from denying any sensation to animals, Descartes therefore gives an account of it. Admittedly, this account is not always as clear as it could be; this is the 'fuzziness' to which Cottingham refers, and the reason why we constantly find different schools of Descartes criticism claiming *both* that animals cannot feel *and* that animals are capable of genuine perceptual cognition. Both statements can be true if 'feeling' is understood as 'a higher-level awareness of one's own sensation' (Descartes's animals do not have this) and 'genuine perceptual cognition' is understood as 'the natural impulses of anger, fear, hunger and so on' (Descartes's animals do have these; AT V, 278). In fairness to Descartes, even today's most up-to-date accounts of animal sentience draw attention to a pervasively unhelpful level of linguistic ambiguity. A recent BBC article on animal consciousness found renowned cognitive scientist Stevan Harnad venting his frustration on the topic: 'The field is replete with weasel words and unfortunately one of those is consciousness [. . .] It is a word that is confidently used by a lot of people, but they all mean something different, and so it is not clear at all what it means'.[23] But it is important to remember that, in one of the clearest statements of all, Descartes is fully able to attribute to animals 'what is commonly called life, or a bodily soul, or organic senses' (AT IX.1, 228).

Moreover, and crucially for our ecocritical purposes, we should note how conspicuous and essential it is that Descartes's account of physiology relies fully on our imbrication with the natural world, because it relies on the spirits that are *everywhere* in the material universe. Being a form of subtle matter, animal spirits exist on a continuum with air and flame. Descartes returns to this continuity again and again: the animal spirits are construed 'like the jets of flame that come from a torch'; they are also 'like a very subtle air or wind' (*Passions of the Soul*, arts. 7–12, AT 11, 332, 335), and we have already seen the extended analogy between the body and a musical organ. The analogical language only functions because air and fluid *really do* move around all bodies. The animal spirits are so tiny, so subtle, that they require figurative, imaginative thinking to explain them, as in the analogies given here, but they are no less material for all that. Susan James quotes from a letter by the artist Nicolas Poussin that is almost exactly contemporary with Descartes's letter to Vorstius: 'The joy that has seized me is so great that it overflows on all sides, like a mountain stream which, after a long drought, fills with more rainwater than it can hold and suddenly bursts its banks' (Letter to Chantelou, 3 November 1643, in Blunt 1964, 81, quoted in James 1997, 263). As James notes, Poussin is not speaking entirely metaphorically, since the torrential rush that he describes is an account of the movement of his own animal spirits. And as she notes further, the body for Descartes and his contemporaries is like an unstable river system, prone to violent floods and tides; and again, this use of language is not just figurative. One's passions *really are*, as James puts it, 'a more-or-less uneasy succession of ebbs and flows' through the channels carved by the spirits (1997, 263). We are a constantly changing configuration and reconfiguration of the paths through which the animal spirits flow (*Passions of the Soul*, arts. 39 and 72, AT XI, 358–359, 381–382); this process starts in utero (letter to Mersenne, 30 July 1640, AT III, 120–121). For Descartes, both the body and the brain are infused with sensory experience: 'plastic' in today's terms, dynamic, malleable, elemental.

[23] www.bbc.co.uk/news/articles/cv223z15mpmo#:~:text=Prof%20Birch's%20team%20found%20that,(Sentience)%20Act%20in%20202. The field of animal sentience research is still characterised by 'foundational controversy over the nature of sentience and the criteria for its attribution, leading to heated debate over the presence or absence of sentience in fish and in invertebrates such as cephalopods (e.g. octopods, squid) and arthropods (e.g. bees, crabs)'. See the Horizon 2020 project, Foundations of Animal Sentience project (ASENT), led by Jonathan Birch, which aims at 'a deeper understanding of how these dimensions of sentience relate to measurable aspects of animal behaviour and the nervous system, and a richer picture of the links between sentience, welfare and the ethical status of animals'. www.lse.ac.uk/cpnss/research/research-projects/animal-minds-group/ASENT. See also Birch 2024.

We know that, for Descartes, an individual human body is unlike an animal body in that it gets an additional definition: it can also be considered as 'all the matter which together is united with the soul of that person' (letter to Mesland, 9 September 1645, AT IV, 166). He inevitably insists on separation as well as continuity between bodies. But it can be salutary to remember that Descartes places us clearly and unambiguously on a God-given continuum with the non-human. Considered as bodies in general, human and non-human animals work in exactly the same way, and the world that they inhabit also inhabits them. We can therefore conclude two things: (a) it makes no sense at all, from Descartes's perspective, to hold that we humans are wholly unlike animals, or to be considered entirely separately from them; and (b) the natural world flows through us all. Nature is not just pure exteriority.

2.3 The *Ego Cogitans* Is at the Centre of Everything

With his work on extended matter, Descartes makes a truly systematic attempt to understand and explain the visible and invisible universe: to 'master' it, in that sense. He is one of the first to do so, and his work on the structure of the earth and planets can be seen as one of the most successful and influential outputs of his natural philosophy. We know that Descartes also prefaces all scientific certainty with the work of the thinking self: having established in the *Discourse on Method* that *I am thinking, therefore I exist* (AT VI, 33), he then needs to move on to the existence of everything else around us. He goes into more detail in his work on the *ego cogitans* in the *Meditations*. If Descartes can prove that God exists, then, he says, it will follow from God's benevolence that the objects that appear clearly and distinctly to us actually exist in the external world. He requires God for certainty, but his proof of God of course relies on his own reasoning. (This is the famous Cartesian Circle; on which see in particular Hatfield in Gaukroger 2006, 122–141.) Descartes's thinking mind is very much at the centre of his philosophical system.

All these efforts, however, come in the broader context of a fundamental shift in ways of thinking about the positionality of humans: the new Copernican theory that the sun is at rest near the centre of the universe, while the earth, spinning on its axis once daily, revolves annually around the sun. This (again quite literal) *decentring* of the earth that human beings inhabit, and the human fragility that results, is sometimes missed by anachronistic accounts of his work that focus purely on an exaltation or glorification of the human. The displacement of the earth was sufficiently novel to put Galileo on trial when he espoused Copernican ideas; hence the fact of the posthumous publication of Descartes's

World, which did the same.[24] For the Catholic Church, 'to affirm that the sun is really located in the centre of the universe [. . .] is a very dangerous thing, not only because it irritates all Scholastic philosophers and theologians, but also because it is damaging to the Holy Faith, because it makes the Holy Scriptures false' (letter from Bellarmine to Father Foscarini, 12 April 1615, in Blackwell 1991, 265). The fragility that Descartes attributes to our cosmos is in fact more radical even than the Copernican impulse, as Gaukroger emphasises: 'Because it has a centre around which the planets and fixed stars revolve, Copernicus' space has an intrinsic directionality, a notion that Descartes definitively rejects' (2002, 139).

Descartes's cosmos, outlined in the *World*'s 'Treatise on Light' and then, in more textbook fashion, in the *Principles*, is made up of an indefinite number of planetary solar systems, with each revolving on its own axis. We know that Descartes's starting point is always that there is no unfilled space; thus, each time a particle moves in space, another must move in to fill the gap, creating a series of interlocking 'vortices', as in the beautiful illustration of contiguity in the firmament in Figure 1.

Each sun in this multiply heliocentric system is at the centre of a vortex of rotating fluid matter, which carries its planets with it. Descartes's mechanistic philosophy means that our own planet is profoundly interconnected with all others. Planets have a 'constant tendency to move in a circular fashion', but, in as much as all the bodies in the universe are contiguous ('s'entre-touchent', in the French translation) and act on one another, 'the motion of any one body depends on the motion of all the others, and hence is subject to countless variations' (*Principles*, part 3, art. 157, AT VIII, 202; AT IX.2, 200 for the French). Planets themselves are born as a by-product of occluded rotating stars, when material caught up in the vortices coalesces. Collision often leads to the breaking up and dividing of parts of matter into the elements of fire and air, but, in the case of bodies whose shapes are 'so extended and sufficiently able to prevent this' (i.e. larger or stronger than the others with which they collide), it is easier for several of them to join together, and in this way to become larger (*The World*, chapter 9, 'On the origin and the course of the planets and comets in general, and of comets in particular', AT XI, 57). Occasionally, planets may be moving so quickly as to be carried outside their own solar system altogether: then, they become comets. As stars, through occlusion, become less and less active, they will be engulfed by the vortices around them; as a result of this, whole solar systems collapse (*Principles*, part 3, arts. 115–119).

[24] In March 1637, in a moment of levity in the correspondence, Descartes reacts to his friend Mersenne's suggestion that killing him would at this point be a good idea, to allow his work to be safely released: AT I, 348.

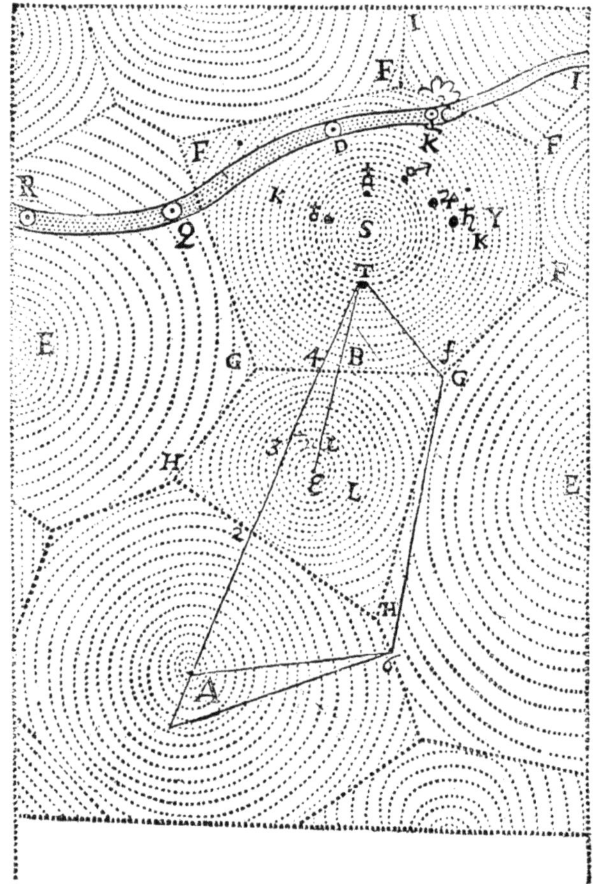

Figure 1 Contiguous matter, from the *Treatise on Light*, chapter 8: 'On the Formation of the Sun and the Stars in this New World' (AT XI, 55)

Descartes might disagree with Pascal on the existence of void space (for a summary of the argument, see Clarke 2003), but he certainly relies heavily on the ideas of infinity and indefiniteness, so that some of his statements end up anticipating the measureless figurations of space that make Pascal a fine theorist of the non-human. In Descartes, there is no imaginable extension that is so great that we cannot understand the possibility of an even greater one, so size is indefinite. Or again, no matter how great we imagine the number of stars to be, we still think that God could have created more, and so the number of stars is indefinite (*Principles*, part 1, art. 16; AT VIII, 15). If the universe is indefinite in this way, God is infinity itself, 'so that nothing can be added to his perfection', as we see in the *Meditations* (AT VII, 47). Thus, the third part of the *Principles* begins with two points, which together powerfully undermine human centrality:

> The first is that we must bear in mind the infinite power and goodness of God, and not be afraid that our imagination may overestimate the vastness, beauty and perfection of his works. [...] The second point is that we must always remember that our mental capacity is very mediocre, and we must beware of having too high an opinion of ourselves. (AT VIII, 80; AT IX.2, 104)

This respect for the infinite is a constant throughout Descartes's oeuvre. At the end of the Third Meditation, his meditator remains for some time 'in the contemplation of God himself, to ponder on his attributes, and to gaze on, wonder at, and worship the beauty of this immense light, as much as the eye of my understanding, shrouded as it is in darkness, is capable of doing' (AT VII, 52).

Descartes's treatment of matter places us and everything visibly around us in the position of tiny specks floating in an unimaginably vast interstellar universe. The constant motion means that nothing is in equilibrium forever. We cannot control or contain the violent processes that surround us. Descartes's attempt to at least understand these processes offers (again quite scandalously, as far as the Roman Inquisition is concerned) absolutely no special privileges to this earth.[25] The human capacity to think, mediocre as it is, will not count for much in the face of the total collapse of our solar system; and this possibility is a logical and explicit consequence of Descartes's account of the world. As Gaukroger summarises:

> Having not only moved the Earth from the centre of the cosmos, but also made it little more than a piece of refuse from another solar system, Descartes puts himself in a position where he can consider it in the same way as any other concentration of solid matter, and indeed can consider any other planet as being like the Earth. (2002, 161)

Our world is one world among others.

2.4 We Can Subjugate Animals as We Wish

The 'doctrine of the animal-machine', strongly associated with Descartes, is often used to introduce the idea that we can subjugate animals to our own ends. However, the term 'animal-machine' itself, expressed in that form and as a 'doctrine', does not make any notable appearance or intervention in his work. It is generally used after his death, to summarise the pages at the end of the *Discourse on Method* and the contents of his *World* – his physics and

[25] Descartes's works were put on the Index of Forbidden Books by the censors of Rome in 1663. Extracts of further condemnations of his works are given in the Appendix in Ariew, Cottingham and Sorell 1998, 252–260.

physiology. In that context, Descartes sets up an analogy between animal and human bodies, as discussed in Section 2.2.[26]

As we have seen, what Descartes's animals cannot do is *think*, where thinking is understood as a higher-order level of self-conscious reflection. Descartes's physiology is run together with his method, which, from the *Discourse* on, is dedicated to dispelling possible doubt and achieving certainty. This kind of certainty is based on the fact that we cannot doubt that we are thinking. 'I am talking to my neighbour', for instance, could be put in doubt: maybe I am dreaming, or, who knows, in the grip of an evil demon who wants me to think that I am talking to my neighbour. But what I cannot doubt is that *I think* I am talking to my neighbour. A dog, on the other hand, would for Descartes respond to the neighbour's dog on a different, physical, pre-reflective (but always basically sentient) level. Doubt, certainty, judgement, and thought do not come into it. Smell, sight, sound, and a wagging of the tail that can be viewed as non-threatening: these are not excluded.

Descartes sets up a rather inadequate proof for his idea that animals, unlike humans, do not possess an immortal, thinking soul. He bases this on the human ability to talk, by which he means our ability to use signs on matters that are not related to our passions (he includes sign language), and therefore to string ideas together in myriad ways, and therefore also to give meaningful responses to unforeseen questions. Parrots can be trained to talk, and animals can communicate their bodily passions to each other and to us. Descartes even sets up the example of a magpie that, when trained to greet its mistress on her approach, feels not just a passion in the immediate (e.g. joy or fear), but an awareness that extends into the future: 'for instance it will be an expression of the hope of eating, if it has always been given a titbit when it says it' (Letter to Newcastle, 23 November 1646, AT IV, 574). But animals cannot talk in a fully, limitlessly interactive way. 'This seems to me', Descartes continues swiftly,

> a very strong argument to prove that the reason why animals do not speak as we do is not that they lack the organs, but that they have no thoughts. It cannot be said that they speak to each other but we cannot understand them; for since dogs and some other animals express their passions to us, they would also express their thoughts if they had any. (Letter to Newcastle, AT IV, 575)

[26] This section speaks particularly closely to Cottingham 1978, and should also be read alongside Kambouchner 2024, which in turn reprises material in Kambouchner 2015 and 2023. In summary there: 'Against the accusation of "speciesism," a hierarchy that considers humans superior and justifies their domination and cruelty towards animals, it is argued that Descartes did not regard animals as completely insensible, that his position was not as categorical as often presented, and that he can be interpreted not as a speciesist but as an environmental advocate' (Kambouchner 2024, 229).

This is a reprisal of the passages from the *Discourse on Method* already encountered, where animal skilfulness, even as it exceeds human capacity in some respects just like the ropes and springs of a clock, does not comprise any 'esprit', or the mental powers of thought (AT VI, 59). Mental powers (the powers of the immortal soul) amount to an infinite combinatorial capacity: the ability to react to the unpredictable, or the unprogrammable, and to come to a judgement accordingly, and to be aware of one's own capacity to do so. If animals could think like humans can, they would be able to do all this and then talk about it. Clearly, when it comes to views on animal–human communication, this 'sets the bar quite high' (Moriarty 2015, 363).

Anyone whose life, or any brief part of it, has been transformed by contact with an animal will no doubt be less convinced than Descartes is himself by the strength of his arguments. 'I rather doubt whether this view can carry conviction in readers' minds', writes Descartes's (nevertheless favoured) correspondent, Antoine Arnauld, as he caustically breaks down a sheep's response to a wolf in mechanistic terms, reducing it to the pattern of light on a retina. Is there really no judgement involved? It is perfectly understandable to assume that there is. Descartes's argument to the contrary would need to be confirmed by 'extremely solid reasons'; and Arnauld implies that those are lacking (Fourth Objections to the *Meditations*, AT IX.1, 159–160). When Descartes attributes to animals 'what is commonly called life, or a bodily soul, or organic senses' (AT IX.1, 228), he is returning to this criticism. In the later letter to More, Descartes further acknowledges that, 'though I regard it as established that we cannot prove that there *is* any thought in animals, I do not think that it is thereby proved that there *is not*, since the human mind does not reach into their hearts' (5 February 1649, AT 5, 276). There is at bottom a very basic level of argumentation at which it just seems improbable to him that worms and flies and caterpillars (or, in the letter to Newcastle, oysters and sponges) can have souls (AT V, 277; AT IV, 576).[27]

Against Descartes's work here we can line up: the fables of La Fontaine, the fairy tales of Charles Perrault or Mme d'Aulnoy, countless examples of salon poetry, various moral tales of animal bravery or cunning or doggedness or charm offered from the perspective of cross-species similarity rather than difference, stories of animals who were once humans, and humans who were once animals, and talking human–animal hybrids, and so on. This rich early modern engagement with non-human animals can be broadly construed as a riposte to Descartes – or, better, it can be tightly construed as a riposte to

[27] For fishes and invertebrates as, in 2024, the 'centre of the debate' on where the 'edge of sentience' is situated, see Birch 2024, chapter 12.

a later, received version of his work, on which more later in this section. One gets a sense in many such texts of hours spent in the company of animals, observing their minute perfections, their complex behaviours. La Fontaine's animals demonstrate, variously, flexibility of mind, inferential reasoning, sophisticated argumentation, and excellent engineering skills. Descartes's niece, Catherine, evokes a small warbler that repeatedly came back to visit her friend, Madeleine de Scudéry, with the following well-placed objection as a line of verse: 'With all due respect to my uncle, she has judgement'.[28] (Catherine has accurately noted that the best line of criticism is to get René on animal judgement, not animal feeling.) Scudéry herself has two pet chameleons, received as a gift from the French Consul in Alexandria in 1672, and pens an observational account that richly details not just their habits but also their affective capacity for friendship (Scudéry 2022).

Meanwhile, Descartes's own observations of animals do not extend much beyond a mention of those 'who scratch the earth for the purpose of burying their excrement; they hardly ever actually bury it, which shows that they act only by instinct and without thinking' (to Newcastle, 23 November 1646, AT IV, 576). Descartes had a dog himself ('Mister Scratch'); he once lent him to his friend and translator, the Abbé Picot, for breeding purposes, sending him with a trusted valet (AT V, 133). But, if he spent his idle hours entranced by his pet, he certainly did not write about it at length for publication, and we are entitled to prefer writers who do.

When Jacques Derrida, for instance, writes his very deliberately titled essay, 'The Animal that Therefore I am', about his experience of being interpellated by his cat while exiting the shower, he is obviously giving himself a contrasting set of priorities, while critiquing all forms of anthropocentrism. He is acknowledging the direct, inquisitorial gaze of the animal and asking what it does to his own sense of self to be, as he puts it, 'seen seen' by this animal, as differentiated from all others (Derrida 2008, 29–30; see Gontier 2010). It is similarly lovely to reach back into the sixteenth century and find Montaigne playing with his own cat: 'When I play with my cat, who knows if I am not a pastime to her more than she is to me? We entertain each other with reciprocal monkey tricks. If I have my time to begin or to refuse, so has she hers'. ('Apologie de Raymond Sebond', in

[28] Madeleine de Scudéry inserts this poem into a letter to Huet from 1689 (Rathery and Boutron 1873, 312–313). The salon environment she frequented has not received the attention it deserves as a locus of learned philosophical reception, and nor has salon poetry always been seen as a valid way of registering a philosophical response. See the project 'Cultures of Philosophy: Women Writing Knowledge in Early Modern Europe' (CultPhil), led by Helena Taylor, which aims to appraise the material, socio-literary, and conceptual conditions for women writing knowledge, and to analyse the reception of such writing: https://culturesofphilosophy.exeter.ac.uk/about/. See also Taylor 2021.

Montaigne 1999, 2, 12, 452 c and Montaigne 2003, 401). We may justifiably prefer Montaigne's suggestive and appealing view, utterly dismissed by Descartes, that the differences between any one human being and another can be greater than those between a human being and an animal.[29] But none of this means that Descartes's animals are feelingless entities to be dominated and subjugated at will. It just means that the behaviour of non-human animals is never his primary focus.

Even the horrifying if extremely widespread practice of vivisection, practised since Aristotle and Galen, needs to be analysed with some intellectual caution in this regard (see Andrault 2022 and 2024). We know that Descartes performed vivisection on fish, frogs, and rabbits (AT IV, 686; AT 1, 523) and at least witnessed it being performed on dogs (AT 11, 241). It is very often claimed (e.g. in Singer 1975, 219) that he thereby popularised vivisection and that his practice of it demonstrates his brutal imperviousness to animal suffering. However much one abhors animal cruelty, such claims often rely on faulty citation, and simply run too quickly over the challenges posed by early modern scientific practice and theory. A significant renewal of the study of anatomy, and with it the exponential multiplication of dissections and vivisections, takes place from the early sixteenth century on (Allen Shotwell 2013); by the 1620s and 1630s, this commonly extends beyond faculties of medicine into the private or semi-private cabinets and studies of *savant* experimentation.

Just as Harvey did when investigating the circulation of the blood in 1628, and as so many of his contemporaries agree is necessary, Descartes recommends the experience of watching and participating in experimentation upon animal anatomy. Even those who do grant souls to animals, such as Pierre Gassendi and Christiaan Huygens, insist on this. The practice was quite simply part of all contemporary debates about the circulation of blood, the digestive system, and sensorimotor functioning. It does not always or necessarily imply a total indifference to animal suffering, and the distinction between a form of manipulation that 'torments' animals and other swifter or more definitive gestures is present and operative (Andrault 2022, para. 23). Even anatomists who present themselves as reluctant to engender animal suffering, indeed appalled by it, think that the ends of scientific utility and respect for *nature as a whole* justify experimentation. This is the case with Thomas Bartholin, who describes himself as so easily moved to pity that only the 'urgent necessity' of observing 'the course of the humours' could possibly justify the process (1655, 96). Whether one sees this as disingenuous or not (Bartholin's own reputation as an anatomist is clearly

[29] See 'De l'inéqualité qui est entre nous' ('Of the inequality that is between us'), in Montaigne 1999, I, 42, 258 and Montaigne 2003, 229; and Descartes to Newcastle, November 23, 1646, AT IV, 573–576.

not absent as a motivating factor), it shows that animal suffering is not the object of systematic denial on the part of early modern vivisectionists. If anything, it is precisely 'because animals resemble us that it seems crucial to take part in this kind of experimentation' (Andrault 2022, para. 34).

We have seen that Descartes does not deny sensation in animals; therefore, he does not deny them pain either, in the most basic sense of a 'sensus', or aversive bodily response. He is making a distinction that bears some prima facie similarity to current distinctions between pain as nociception on the one hand and affective experience involving 'valence and arousal' on the other (for which distinction, see Birch 2024, 34–35). When Descartes writes to Mersenne that pain is experienced 'dans l'entendement', or 'in the understanding' (11 June 1640, AT III, 85), he is defining 'feeling pain' in his own very reflexive way, as something like 'I am aware of this pain that I am feeling and I need to do something about it'. With this restriction, animals do not experience 'la douleur proprement dite': pain 'properly understood' (AT III, 85). We can take it therefore that they do experience pain 'improperly' or loosely understood: an unpleasant sensation on the level of the body. This must be analogous to the 'natural impulses' of fear, hunger, and so on, directly attributed to animals in the letter to More (AT V, 278), but not quite on the level of the 'perception' of those impulses, which Descartes describes in the responses to the sixth objections (AT IX.1, 236). Unsurprisingly, and as we have seen all along, the distinction has not been easy to work with. 'Please note that I am speaking of thought', Descartes still has to insist to More in 1649, not long before his death, 'and not of life and sensation [*de cogitatione, non de vita, vel sensu*]' (AT V, 278).

His is not a position that promotes cruelty towards animals, continues Descartes to More at the close of this same letter, while nevertheless noting that it does allow humans to kill animals for food (just as it correspondingly allows for scientific experimentation on animals). The practice of vegetarianism is here dismissed as 'superstition', in that it is seen as the product of a belief in reincarnation, or the transmigration of souls across species, familiar in the period from Pythagoras's speech in book 15 of Ovid's *Metamorphoses*: 'Therefore, my opinion is not cruel to wild beasts, but rather favourable to men, whom, unless they are followers of the superstition of the Pythagoreans, it absolves of the suspicion of crime in eating or killing animals' (AT V, 278–279). Descartes is allowing for a distinction that is still the fundamental basis of animal rights legislation today: between (a) the (entirely commonplace) killing of animals for the benefit of humans, including for food, and (b) cruelty, or the gratuitous causing of suffering. Readers may well prefer to conflate those two categories; this is beyond Descartes's scope. He can be accused again of a broader lack of interest: he does not engage critically, in a sustained or imaginative way, with animal responsiveness or behaviour or moral standing. But, as he clearly says, life consists in the heat of the heart, and sensation depends on the bodily organs. Human and non-human animals share flesh, blood, and bone, and are therefore vulnerable to physical violence.

The reception of Descartes's work on animals became all the more trenchant from the 1660s on, with the posthumous publication of the two treatises that make up his *World*: the *Treatise on Man* (which appeared in Latin in 1662) and the *Treatise on Light* (which appeared in French in 1664). Thereafter, the extracts of Descartes's major texts discussed here were taken up by other Cartesian thinkers who *did* want to construe the absence of an animal soul to mean that animals lack feeling or responsiveness or sentience of any kind. A crucial role was played by Florentius Schuyl's preface to his Latin translation of the *Treatise on Man*. This offered an expansive discussion of the animal as machine, in the local context of 'a polemical engagement with the church in society, the definition of religious orthodoxy, and the correct interpretation of the Bible', specifically the Bible on animals (Vermij 2023, 194). The term 'animal-machine' or 'beast-machine', as shorthand for a coherent doctrine, starts appearing regularly in the subsequent reception. Schuyl's preface is a good example of how the phenomenon of 'Cartesianism' often arose in specific polemical situations, rather than as a neutrally philosophical engagement with Descartes. Another good example is the development of the legend that Descartes constructed an automaton of his daughter, now often used to strengthen an account of his role as a dehumanising 'proto-cybernetic theorist' (Kang 2017, 637). As Kang has shown in an excellent reconstruction of the reception history, this emerged from a brief account of a 'zealous Cartesian' who wished to defend Descartes against the allegation that he had conceived a daughter out of wedlock (as in fact he had), by claiming that there was only ever a mechanical version. The fictional mechanical daughter displaces the real one, and has done ever since.

In one of the most influential instances of the reception of Descartes, Nicolas Malebranche's *De la recherche de la verité* or *Concerning the Search After Truth* (1674–1675) famously embraces a strong version of mechanism and animal automatism. When he says that animals 'eat without pleasure' and 'cry without pain', he denies them feeling on any level whatsoever (1945, vol. 2, book 6, 255). Even he claims that human compassion can and should put a useful brake on animal cruelty (1945, vol. 1, book 2, 121), although a later anecdote about him kicking a dog suggests that, reputationally at least, this compassion was placed on the level of theory rather than practice (Trublet 1759, 115). From 1690, the definition of cruelty towards animals as 'Cartesian' is so embedded that it can be the object of pastiche, as in Gabriel Daniel's anti-Cartesian narrative, *Voyage du monde de Descartes* (1690, 356–357 and 1692, 241):

> Before my Conversion to *Cartesianism,* I was so pitiful and Tender-hearted, that I could not so much as see a Chicken kill'd: But since I was once persuaded that Beasts were destitute both of Knowledg and Sense, scarce a Dog in all the Town, wherein I was, could escape me, for the making *Anatomical* Dissections, wherein I my self was *Operator,* without the least inkling of Compassion or Remorse.

The Port-Royal thinker Nicolas Fontaine, underlining his own teacher's humanity in contrast to the Cartesian circle of the Duc de Luynes, also testifies that the influence of Cartesian ideas could be taken as a flippant justification for abuse:

> There was hardly a man who was not talking about *automata.* No-one thought anything of whipping a dog. They administered these beatings with great indifference, and made fun of those who pitied the creatures as if they felt pain. They said the animals were clocks; that the cries they emitted when struck were only the noise of a little spring that had been pressed, but that the whole thing was without feeling. They nailed these poor animals up on boards by their four paws in order to vivisect them and see the circulation of blood which was a great subject of conversation. (Fontaine 1738, 74)

There is no reason to think of these accounts as exaggerated in this, also the era of bear-baiting, cockfighting, and so on. Such 'sport' had been common for centuries but was now big business across Europe: a hotly ticketed 'carnival of cruelty'.[30] There were detractors, just as there were vegetarians, or 'Pythagoreans' (Borlik 2009). After a visit to the Bear Gardens in June 1670, the English diarist John Evelyn recorded a day of 'butcherly sports, or rather barbarous cruelties' and declared himself 'most heartily weary of the rude and dirty pastime' (2015, 307). And the wealth of animal tales mentioned earlier in this section surely counters an indifference to non-human beings in the broader cultural context too. Nevertheless, it is clearly the case that many seventeenth-century responses to 'Descartes' were also responding specifically to a version of his work that had already become simplified, polemical, satirical, or all of these at once:

[30] In the British context, Dickey considers the torment of animals and theatrical performance as 'culturally isomorphic events' (Dickey 1991, 255–256), and increasingly prestigious ones at that. On 25 May 1559, for example, a French delegation to London was 'brought to Court with musick to dinner, and after a splendid dinner, they were entertained with the baiting of bears and bulls with English dogs. The Queen's Grace herself and the Ambassadors stood in the gallery looking on the pastime till six at night' (Nichols 1823, 67–68).

> So they say
> That the beast is a machine;
> That in it all passes without choice and by springs
> No feeling, no soul; in it all is body.
> Such is the watch that carries on,
> With steps always equal, blind and without intent.
> ('Discourse addressed to Mme de la Sablière', in La Fontaine 1923, 240)

By the time La Fontaine writes these verses in book 9 of his *Fables*, published in 1679, such descriptions of Descartes's views are well and truly entrenched.

Amid all Descartes's many successes, his writing about animals can be considered a failure. As Antoine Arnauld predicted in 1641 (AT IX.1, 159), it does not easily 'carry conviction': it is lacunary, de-emphasises animal behaviour and sociality, and fails to anticipate fully that it could be used to disregard animal sentience. Having separated mortal, living bodies from the immortal thinking mind, it was simply too easy for Descartes's readers to forget about the 'mortal, living' part. For Riskin, 'the possibility that Descartes laboured to introduce, the possibility that matter contained life but not soul, became virtually inconceivable in the philosophical, theological, cultural, and political moment he was struggling to define' (2016, 69). Descartes's own positive attribution to animals of 'what is commonly called life, or a bodily soul, or organic senses' (AT IX.1, 228) seems to have been too little, too late, too ineffectual.

2.5 We Can Master and Possess Nature as a Whole

In part 3 of the *Principles*, Descartes tackles the idea of human instrumentalisation head-on: 'And it would be the height of presumption if we were to imagine that all things were created by God for our benefit alone, or even to suppose that the power of minds can grasp the ends which he set before himself in creating the universe' (*Principles*, part 3, art. 2, AT VIII, 81). How can this possibly fit with the renowned statement in the *Discourse on Method* that, 'knowing the power and action of fire, water, air, stars, the heavens, and all the other bodies that are around us as distinctly as we know the different trades of our craftsmen, we could put them to all the uses for which they are suited and thus make ourselves as it were the masters and possessors of nature' (AT VI, 62)?

As suggested in Section 1, we can only answer this question by reading around those keywords, 'mastery' and 'possession', which almost always appear in isolation. First, we can think about what comes before: an analogy with 'the different trades of our craftsmen'. The idea of craft and artisanal production brings in a sense of harnessing to scale. In the Abbé Picot's French translation of the *Principles*, enthusiastically received by Descartes, the machines of craftsmen 'always have to be in some proportion to the hands of those that make them' (part 4, art. 203, AT IX.2, 321). In the *Discourse*, the ideas of proportionality and appropriate use are strongly salient: we could put the bodies around us to all the uses for which they are suited (*à tous les usages auxquels ils sont propres*, AT VI, 62). In other words, we could use our knowledge of the natural world *for all the purposes for which it is appropriate*. Thus, 'Descartes' remark need not imply that we should also be lords and masters in the sense that we should exploit nature for our own (selfish) needs and purposes' (Wee 2001, 285). This would not be appropriate. The universe does not exist for our benefit alone.

Further, we need also to understand that the main direction of travel in this paragraph is a consideration of how physics can develop into medicine. Descartes does anticipate the 'discovery of a host of inventions which will lead us effortlessly to enjoy the fruits of the earth and all the commodities that can be found in it' (AT VI, 62), but this projected enjoyment, which alone sounds rather fanciful, comes in the context of 'the preservation of health, which is without doubt the highest good and the foundation of all other goods in this life' (AT VI, 62). The overall goal is futuristic, hypothetical: we *could perhaps* one day do this, and Descartes explains later that he is thinking about a timeframe stretching over 'several centuries' (AT IX.2, 20). This is also a quite standard summary of the long-term plans underlying the 'scientific revolution' as a whole: mechanistic philosophy may eventually relieve the suffering of humanity, and medicine will give us strength. These lines, writes Denis Kambouchner, 'must be read in the opposite sense from the standard reading': that is, not as a brand-new ambition, but as an allusion to the hopes and large-scale aspirations of an entire body of work that is dominating Descartes's intellectual world (Kambouchner 2023, 261). This body of work proceeds in turn from a basic assumption about the shortness and precariousness of human lives.

The new science in which Descartes is participating often stresses, at its very origin and source, human inadequacy – the *fall* of man. As Harrison (2007, 258) puts it, 'The birth of modern experimental science was not attended with a new awareness of the powers and capacities of human reason, but rather the opposite – a consciousness of the manifold deficiencies of the intellect, of the misery of the human condition, and of the limited scope of scientific achievement.' Thus, Francis Bacon's project to reform philosophy in 1620 was motivated by an attempt to determine whether the human mind 'might by any means be restored to its perfect and original condition, or if that may not be, yet reduced to a better condition than that in which it now is' (Bacon 1857–1874, IV, 7). This goal persists across the seventeenth century. In London, Bacon's intellectual heirs formed the Royal Society, where Robert

Hooke, in 1665, would commence his sensational study of the microscopic natural world as follows: 'And as at first, mankind fell by tasting of the forbidden Tree of Knowledge, so we, their Posterity, may be in part restor'd by the same way, not only by beholding and contemplating, but by tasting too those fruits of Natural knowledge, that were never yet forbidden' (Hooke 1665, preface [n.p.]) Descartes's reference to our enjoyment of the fruits of the earth is participating in this same semantic field of fallenness, failure, and an inevitably partial restoration.

Descartes's own project, in its self-professed originality, does of course diverge from many aspects of these developments. He rejects any specific theological orientation, and is silent on the Bible in general, given the pressing need to stay out of religious controversy, as vividly evidenced by the arrest of Galileo in 1633. He also rejects (from 1628, when he moved to the Netherlands) the atmosphere of communal learned sociability, though correspondence remains vital throughout his life. But he certainly shares the desire to create a revolution that will abandon the vain learning of the Schools, which had far too readily assumed that knowledge of nature could be gathered with ease, as in the 'confident, assuming and dogmatic school of Aristotle' (Bacon 1857–1874, IV, 672).

It is worth stressing too that the slim volume that we associate today with the 'possession of nature' is quite unlike the chunky material text of the original. In their specific and local context, the final sections of the *Discourse on Method* are mainly designed to serve as a prolegomenon to three scientific writings, the *Dioptrics*, the *Meteors*, and the *Geometry*, with which the *Discourse* was initially published in 1637. Descartes's emphasis in that text and beyond is always on this future-oriented deduction from general principles, and on the boldness of his own scientific enterprise – in which each element has to be confirmed by clarity, distinctness, and evidence as a reliable building-block for further deductions. This is not pure empiricism, science through experiment alone; but Descartes always wants that reason should 'accord so perfectly with experiment', as he puts it in the work on rainbows in the *Meteors*, that it is not possible for us to doubt our own explanations (AT VI, 334). Respect for scientific experiment, and for the experience we gain through it, is built into his work as into that of his contemporaries, and the wisdom we achieve will in turn assist our further investigations of the body, ameliorating 'innumerable diseases, both of the body and of the mind', and perhaps alleviating 'the infirmities of old age' (AT VI, 62). This, again, is the confirmed purpose of Descartes's push towards mastery: a temporally extended life, in an environment where so much works against that. Since 'the mind depends so much on the temperament and disposition of the bodily organs', we need to find some systematic way of making humans 'in general wiser and more skilful than they have been until now' (AT VI, 62).

The reference to the 'fruits of the earth' also points beyond the many scientific writings, to Descartes's later work and his preface to the French translation of his *Principles*, where another organic metaphor is crucial:

> The whole of philosophy is like a tree, the roots of which are metaphysics and the trunk physics, while the branches that grow from the trunk are all the other sciences, which may be reduced to three principal ones, namely, medicine, mechanics and ethics (by which I mean the highest and most perfect ethics), which, since it presupposes a comprehensive knowledge of the other sciences, is the ultimate degree of wisdom. (AT IX.2, 14)

Again, a form of wisdom is sketched out that reveres knowledge as an outgrowth: a growing, changing thing. The very comparison of philosophy to a tree gives the discipline a kind of animate generality. And the idea that this can also encompass a clear respect for the natural world also comes across strongly in an important letter to Elisabeth of Bohemia, in which Descartes expressly sums up all his philosophy thus far. We need to dissipate the very ground of human superiority, to 'form a proper judgement of the works of God, and to come to terms with the vast idea of the extent of the universe that I have attempted to convey in book III of the Principles of Philosophy' (5 September 1645, AT 4, 292). For if we wrongly imagine, he continues,

> that beyond the heavens, there is nothing, only imaginary space, and that the heavens themselves were created only for the service of the earth, and the earth only for man, this encourages us to think that this earth is our principal dwelling place, and this life the best we have; and instead of getting to know the perfections that truly exist within ourselves, we falsely attribute imperfections to other creatures, in order to raise ourselves up above them [...]. (AT IV, 292)

Here, as in the summary of mechanism discussed in Section 2.2, Descartes uncovers layers of divine perfection in both the human and the non-human. Although each of us is a person separate from other people, and whose interests are in some sense distinct from everybody else's, 'we should nonetheless bear in mind that we cannot exist on our own, and that each of us is, in fact, part of the universe' (AT IV, 293).

There is of course the opposing narrative in Genesis, that God made everything for our benefit, and Descartes acknowledges this in a letter to Chanut: 'Preachers, whose concern is to spur us on to the love of God, commonly lay before us the various benefits we derive from other creatures and say that God made them for us' (6 June 1647, AT V, 55).[31] Nevertheless, we cannot say that all things are made for our sake, since, in fact, it is clearly the case that 'all things are made for his [God's] sake', because 'God alone is the final as well as the efficient cause of the universe' (AT V, 53). Insofar as created beings, in Descartes's letter, are 'of service to each other, any of them may ascribe to itself a privileged position and consider that all those useful to it are made for its sake' (AT V, 54). This shift of perspective supposes that *each and every* creature can see itself at the centre of its own universe. It makes essentially the same point as Montaigne playing with his cat (or is his cat playing with him?) – though Descartes is inevitably more serious in tonality (see earlier, Section 2.4, and Kambouchner 2023, 271–272).

This same letter to Chanut returns us to the discussion of the human inability to perceive limits to the universe, and even goes so far as to countenance life forms on other planets:

> If the indefinite extension of the universe gives grounds for inferring that there must be inhabitants of places other than the earth, so does the extension which all the astronomers attribute to it; for every one of them judges that the earth is smaller in comparison with the entire heavens than a grain of sand in comparison with a mountain. (AT V, 56)[32]

In that sense, and in Descartes's scientific worldview, human beings as we know them are comprehensively decentred. In the end, the universe always masters us.

2.6 Human Action Can and Should Be Performed with Total Rational Control

We might not be able to understand God's plans, or the indefinite extent of the universe, but the idea of rational control is obviously crucial to Descartes and his philosophical system. From his earliest philosophical statements on, Descartes wants to direct his thoughts in a controlled way. He starts by rejecting all beliefs open to doubt; he finds the statement 'I am thinking, therefore I exist' to be the first principle for his new philosophy; he concludes from the Cogito that he is essentially a thinking thing (a soul distinct from the body); he wants to generalise from this experience of certainty to say that whatever we can conceive with the same degree of clarity and distinctness is true. This is the kind of certainty we are looking for. When he writes his *Meditations*, he gives

[31] For a modern example of a Christian theological perspective that aims at a robust defence of animal rights beyond the human stewardship of the natural world, see Linzey 2016. For comparative religious viewpoints, see Birch 2024, sections 4.5 and 4.6.

[32] See also the Conversation with Burman, AT V, 168, for the same point.

them the title 'Meditations on First Philosophy', because the book deals 'not specifically with God and the soul, but in general with all the first things we can know by philosophizing' (to Mersenne, 11 November 1640, AT III, 235). So, he is trying to create a firm foundation for *scientia*. And Descartes does not just deal with *what we know*, but also with *how we judge* – judgement being the action of the will upon an idea – and increasingly, as he approaches the ethical branches on the tree of philosophy, with how we ought to behave when acting on our judgement. Virtue is using all the powers of our mind to attain a correct judgement; and satisfaction, he will say repeatedly, is further judging that we have done so.

This controlled, Cartesian virtue is famously summed up in relation to one particular quality, defined in article 153 of the *Passions of the Soul*: *la générosité*. Cartesian generosity, often translated as 'nobility of soul', is a firm and constant resolution to use one's free will well, which makes the generous person master their passions perfectly. In the *Passions*, in which Descartes makes the interaction of mind and body his central focus, he explains 'the passions in general' in part 1, considers their 'number and order' in part 2, and takes particular passions in detail in part 3, with the overall goal of successful management. The task of regulation, if performed successfully, will itself bring joy (art. 212).

Descartes therefore returns to a detailed exploration of the way that animal spirits move around our bodies, carving channels in them as we respond to perceptions. Thus, passions in the soul are excited, via the animal spirits, by 'the subject that acts most immediately upon it', that is 'the body to which it is united' (art. 2). These passions are not always easy to understand or read, as a brief glimpse of the contradictory titles of articles 114–116 reveals: 'How joy causes blushing' (114); 'How sadness causes pallor' (115); 'How it is that we often blush when sad' (116). The early modern literary fascination with fluid, sensuous energy, with how emotions play out on the surface of bodies – sudden changes of colour, the transfixion of a glance – is a thoroughly Cartesian phenomenon. When, in her novel *La Princesse de Clèves* (1678), Mme de Lafayette repeatedly explores her heroine's physical responses, her flushed skin, and her slight micro-gestures, she is engaging in a sustained fictional exploration of the difficult legibility of the passions. Nevertheless, control remains the overall goal of *The Passions of the Soul*, and the soul can work on the body just as the body works on the soul, via the two-way access point that is the pineal gland. If we are afraid, for instance, we can think bold thoughts that will produce the contrary passion of boldness (art. 45); we can also, with resolve, train ourselves to do this more regularly.

Thus it is that true *générosité*,

> in virtue of which a man esteems himself as highly as he may legitimately do, consists in two things and two only: first, he recognises that there is nothing that legitimately belongs to him, save this freedom to direct his acts of will, and that there is no reason why he should be praised or blamed except for his good or bad use of it; secondly, he feels in himself a firm and constant resolution to make good use of it, that is, never to lack the willpower to undertake and execute whatever he judges to be best. (Art. 153)

This is a strong and gendered terminology that has long seemed to fit with the view that Descartes is only interested in the directing agency of a purely masculine reason. Nevertheless, there is and always has been a strong set of feminist responses to Descartes noting, in fact, a quality of openness. 'For since GOD has given Women as well as Men intelligent Souls, why should they be forbidden to improve them?', as Mary Astell puts it (1694, 22). The whole point of the *Passions of the Soul* is that 'nobility of soul can be acquired' (this is the title of art. 161). Various social facts might mean that it is easier for men and people of higher social standing to acquire it, but in theory (and Descartes can sound snobbish in practice), the work of the intellect requires the complete rejection of that conventional reality. For Descartes, one certainly cannot (or should not) take a gendered body, or one bearing the trappings of social class or any other marker of difference, and assume from that anything at all about the superiority or inferiority of the mind.

In this connection, Descartes's respect for the controlled reasoning of his female correspondents is never in doubt. 'I set far more store by her judgments', he writes of Elisabeth, 'than by that of those learned doctors whose rule is to accept the truth of Aristotle's views rather than the evidence of reason' (Descartes to Pollot, 6 October 1642; AT III, 577). He similarly claims of Christina of Sweden that she 'possesses more knowledge, more intelligence and more reason than all the learned churchmen and academics' (Descartes to Brasset, 23 April 1649; AT V, 350). Descartes's anti-scholastic mission, setting store by the common sense that is available to all, has the effect of fully recognising women as philosophical subjects (Pellegrin 2019). This is brought out very clearly in the comprehensively feminist works of his reader François Poulain de la Barre (1647–1725): *De l'égalité des deux sexes* (On the Equality of the Two Sexes) in 1673; *De l'éducation des dames* (On the Education of Ladies) in 1674; and *De l'excellence des hommes* (On the Excellence of Men) in 1675. Poulain 'profoundly changes the panorama of Cartesianism in the second half of the seventeenth century' (Pellegrin 2019, 577). In a dialogue with 'Eulalie', who wishes to improve her own education, he writes, 'If you want to read the Principles of Descartes, and the first volume of his letters written to the Queen of Sweden, and to the Princess of Bohemia, this will still be best. You will see by these letters that he did not judge women incapable of the highest sciences' (Poulain 2021, 272).[33] Reason and the virtue of rational control are open to everyone.

Furthermore, even the emphasis on firmness and constancy in *la générosité* brings with it a problematisation of the idea of *total* control, and a concomitant valorisation of humility. We are bound up with our passions in unpredictable ways. From the title on, article 153, entitled 'In what generosity consists', is closely paralleled in both form and content by article 155, entitled 'In what virtuous humility consists'. Descartes writes:

> The most noble of soul are customarily the most humble; and virtuous humility consists purely in this: in the light of our reflection on the infirmity of our nature, and on the wrongful acts we may have committed in the past, or which we are capable of committing, which are no less serious than those that may be committed by other people, we do not rate ourselves higher than anyone else. (Art. 155)

Again there is an understanding of commonality. It is a basic and fundamental tenet of Descartes's philosophy that, since all other people have free will no less than he or his readers do, they can make just as good use of it. Even so, *making good use of it* is a difficult and precarious enterprise:

> I have included among these remedies the forethought and diligence through which we can correct our natural faults by striving to separate within ourselves the movements of the blood and spirits from the thoughts to which they are usually joined. But I must admit that there are few people who have sufficiently prepared themselves in this way for all the contingencies of life. (Art. 211)

To say that we (unlike animals) possess a soul, a rational soul that can be guided by knowledge of the truth, is perfectly consistent with the idea that we are not very good at using it, on account of the resistance that the world offers. The channels carved by the animal spirits also correspond to the patterns of our previous responses to events. The body's reaction to a new circumstance or impression may vary depending on the situation; but it remains essentially a habitual reaction, determined by corporeal memory that constitutes a part of the 'disposition of the brain', as Descartes puts it (art. 36; see Kambouchner

[33] His advice is good. Critical perspectives that equate Descartes with the masculinisation of thought and science, including environmental science, are still today based upon a very partial characterisation: a preference for the *Discourse* and *Meditations* over the later work and the correspondence (Pellegrin 2019, 577). There is still no complete English-language translation of the correspondence (see Descartes 2024b for a landmark volume 1).

2019, 202). Even if the soul, in Descartes, is free, it can very easily be incited by the passions to react in a particular way. This is one of the main reasons we might choose to assent to things that we do not clearly and distinctly perceive to be true; and one of the reasons why error occurs despite our efforts to forestall it (Meditation 4, AT VII, 52–62).

Descartes's favoured interlocutor, Elisabeth of Bohemia, works to deepen his thinking on error. She points out that often, when he is writing about the attempt to 'investigate the origin and causes of our errors and to learn to guard against them' (*Principles* part 1, art. 31, AT VIII, 17), what he is *really* thinking about is narrating a subsequent response: something like 'I did the best I could'. Even if mistakes are made, she writes, 'You will say that we can still be satisfied, whenever our conscience bears witness that we have taken all possible precautions' (13 September 1645, AT IV, 289). And even if we recognise, as Descartes recommends (see Section 2.5), that we are all part of a bigger whole, and should always put the interests of the whole above our own, 'One who is naturally arrogant will always tip the balance in his own favour, and a modest person will value himself at less than his worth' (30 September 1645, AT IV, 303). She is (of course) right about this, and Descartes's thoughts on virtuous humility seem to constitute his direct response. Beset by ill-health throughout her life and living in exile, Elisabeth is fascinated by the mind–body union that is explored, at her own instigation, in the *Passions*. She steers Descartes's ethical thinking, forcing him to think relationally, and about care, and vulnerability. This brings out a point that is present across his work: there is no possibility at all of the soul *always* being obeyed by the lively, mortal body-machine.

Descartes wants, evidently, to retain a space of liberty for the rational soul. If we are lost in a forest, we need to walk as straight as possible in one direction (AT VI, 24–25). If life throws obstacles in our way, we need to make a decision and stick to it. And yet, even when he is writing within the domain of metaphysics, and certainly within the domain of ethics, Descartes's language twists and turns. 'I know very well', he writes to Elisabeth, 'that it would be imprudent to wish joy on a person to whom fortune sends new sources of dissatisfaction every day, and I am not one of those cruel philosophers who defines a wise man as an insensitive being' (18 May 1645, AT IV, 201–202). His own emphasis on firm intention, on rational control, does not give a full account of the tone of his work. In this and in many other ways, his work deserves to be contextualised within a broader early modern literary culture whose poetic theory also explores patterns of beliefs, intentions, and behaviour; the failure of those patterns; and the language we use to describe them (Gilby 2019). Descartes's intention to persuade the reader to consistent clarity is paralleled by his awareness that individual thought processes are unruly, not least because our bodies are all, in practice, situated in society and in a natural world that treats us unpredictably. The world offers its own resistance as well as the possibility of joy. In this, as in all the preceding discussion, Descartes acknowledges a thick fabric of relations and associations between people and their environments: the actualising power of the world around, and the spirits within.

2.7 The Soul's Only Function Is to Think

Nothing said thus far invalidates the central point. Descartes conceives of human beings as thinking things: uniquely among the living entities of the world, they possess a soul, and the soul's function is to think. Speaking precisely, says his meditator (and precision is his overarching goal): 'I am only a thinking thing, that is a mind, or a soul, or an intellect, or a reason' (AT VII, 27). Before being prompted by Elisabeth, Descartes by his own admission says 'virtually nothing' on the fact that the soul, being united to the body, can act on the body and be acted on along with it (21 May 1643, AT III, 664). This is because he has concentrated very deliberately on the soul's first property, which is that it thinks. Hence the hierarchy inherent in the dialogue of the second Meditation: 'What therefore am I? A thinking thing. What is that? I mean a thing that doubts, that understands, that affirms, that denies, that wishes to do this and does not wish to do that, and also that imagines and perceives by the senses' (AT VII, 28). It is hard not to see the 'and also' here as introducing an ultimately secondary set of considerations. The fact remains, and will always remain, that Descartes wants at bottom to search for truth, to achieve certainty in the sciences.

Even in this final analysis, faced with the unshakeable truth of Descartes's privileging of the rational soul, it is not just possible but also desirable to see his philosophy in terms of a new reckoning of scale. Descartes wants his reader to go on a pedagogical journey with him: 'I wrote Meditations, rather than Disputations, as philosophers normally do, or Theorems and Problems, in the manner of geometers, so that by this fact alone I might make clear that I have no business except with those who are prepared to make the effort to meditate along with me and to consider the subject attentively' (AT VII, 157). As we have seen, he asks that we forget long-held habits of thought and think about thinking in an entirely new way. Knowledge is not to be sought by getting to grips with a range of critical authorities; instead, he asks for an individual search conducted along the precise methodological lines that he lays out. Nevertheless, the work of the pure intellect is only a fractional part of the lives we actually lead.

The hierarchy that Descartes sets up is crucial, with the thinking mind at its apex, but he also inverts it himself. He inverts it, strikingly, when it comes to calculating the time that we should spend on the different activities associated with the soul. He states that he has never spent more than 'a very few hours per year' on the kind of thinking that occupies the intellect alone. This compares to 'a very few hours a day on thoughts that occupy the imagination' (to Elisabeth, 28 June 1643, AT III, 692). Because Descartes situates the imagination within the pineal gland, the locus of the interaction of body and soul via the animal spirits, it is also a hybrid faculty, between sensation and thinking. It can both contemplate 'the shape or image of a bodily thing' (AT VII, 28) and reproduce those figures and images in their absence, in the same or in a modified form (e.g. chimeras or hippogriffs). It is crucial to maintaining and regulating our bodies in a state of health, because we can choose to turn our imagination away from things that cause us harm, as also when we control our passions more generally. This is analogous to – and indeed should be accompanied by – 'medical remedies to thin out the part of the blood that causes obstructions; for which purpose, I judge that Spa water is very suitable' (to Elisabeth, May or June 1645, AT IV, 220).

Indeed, although Descartes believes that it is fully necessary to have understood the principles of metaphysics once in one's life, because they give us the knowledge of God and our soul, he also believes 'that it would be very harmful to occupy one's understanding with frequent meditation on them, because it would then be less at liberty to attend to the functions of the imagination and the senses' (AT III, 695). To attune to the world around is to create the conditions of possibility for the natural philosophy that Descartes values. Even so, he says that the remainder of his time – and we understand therefore that this is the *vast majority* of his time – he has devoted to 'giving my senses and my mind a rest' (AT III, 693). This priority is, again, consistent with the goals of his science, because the health of one's body, as it moves in the world, precedes all other goals.

Elisabeth knows the perils of ill-health well, as mentioned; and at this point in his writing, Descartes is acknowledging the many and various difficulties that his correspondent is facing. One cannot avoid dealing with these domestic difficulties, he agrees. But they cannot be tackled head on, because they are simply too powerful: 'True reason does not command us to challenge them head on and to try to drive them away' (May or June 1645, AT IV, 218). Instead, Descartes sets up a therapy of diversion. Our imagination can work with our understanding to direct the volitions of the soul at healthful objects. There are situations that are so sickening that they force a passive suffering and block an alert response: in the *Passions*, Descartes names a few of these appalling scenarios, as he conjures up the crimes committed in the name of religion (art. 190). But if we can counter such horror with therapeutic techniques, in order to allow us to go on living, then we must. The key example that Descartes gives to Elisabeth comes with the greenness of the natural world. As well as following the usual recommendations of her doctors to mitigate the bad effects of sadness on the temperament of the blood, she should 'avoid any kind of serious meditation on intellectual matters, and instead concentrate on doing the same as those people who, when they gaze at the green of a wood, the colours of a flower, the flight of a bird, and such things as require no attention, convince themselves that they are thinking of nothing' (AT IV, 220).

Descartes's formulation is interesting here, since strictly speaking it is not possible, according to his own protocol, to 'think of nothing'. The closest one can get is a self-reflexive awareness that one is enjoying the relaxation of one's own mind, through a shift in scale and focus. In the name of stillness, Descartes is in fact sketching out the gradual movements and gestures involved, as he tries to create in his reader a readiness to change perspective. One can cast one's eyes over the organic contours of a forest, or gaze minutely at the different colours that go to make up the petals of a flower, or turn one's head, if only very slightly, to follow the flight of a bird. Attention is not blocked or stopped, but modulated.

If we are following, the bird is leading, granted, at this most therapeutic moment of Descartes's oeuvre, a kind of agency of its own. The patterns traced out in flight, aleatory to us only because they are directed by the bird, are at the very edge of the limits of our own awareness. Thus, the bird allows a gestural interplay of outstanding corrective benefit. Descartes's pastoral lexicon invokes not just ease but also a renewal, and a realignment. It connects to the benefits brought by the 'first passion of all', wonder, where the act of wondering at something can 'induce the soul to consent and contribute to those actions that serve either to preserve the body or render it more perfect in some way' (art. 137, AT XI, 430). Too much wonder is a bad thing: it leads to fixation or obsession. One fixes one's attention 'only on objects as they first appear' (art. 78, AT XI, 386), and the forward movement of attention is curtailed. But in moderation, and with the help of the imagination, the local meanderings of our attentiveness are encouraged: 'That is not wasting time, but using it well; for one can in the meantime have the satisfaction of hoping in this way to recover perfect health, which is the foundation of all the other goods that one can have in this life' (AT IV, 220).

The soul is a thinking thing, but we need to take seriously the form of environmental awareness that shines through. The limits of human thinking power are entangled with the vitality of the world around us. The tree of philosophy only flourishes if we acknowledge this; and only if full weight is given to these environmental considerations can we begin to glimpse the emancipatory potential of the thinking soul. Even then, we 'are joined to a mortal and fragile body, subject to many infirmities, and which must inevitably perish in a few years' (to Elisabeth, 18 May 1645, AT IV, 202). In the end, Descartes articulates the meaning of the world and all its many living networks, in all their subtle matter and their infinite wonder, beyond a strictly human perspective.

3 Conclusion

Just as work in the humanities has identified that our place in the natural world ought to be given the highest critical priority, so it has become a commonplace that Descartes's philosophy gave rise to, indeed justified, much that is wrong about attitudes to the non-human environment. Descartes's work is seen as a turning point, or a rupture: we have characterised it as such, and so it has become. He encourages this himself, of course, with his radical statements of intent, his rejection of the power of prior argument, and his thoroughgoing dismissal of his own education. It is tempting to take these mission statements as the beginning and end, the be-all and end-all, of his work. Nevertheless, the direction of travel in studies of Descartes now is always to consider interconnection and continuity alongside individual ambition and estrangement: a return to a pre-canonical Descartes, whose vast network of correspondence makes a major philosophical contribution in itself, who takes elements from the thinkers he rejects (Ariew 2011) while contributing to the flourishing of other schools of thought, and whose work actually serves to *question* the later cultural absorption of Cartesian thinking. So, too, it is possible, I have argued, for environmental thinking and Cartesian philosophy to refine and nourish each other.

The ecohistorical approach that I have advocated here has sought to think its way into locally salient artefacts, ideas, and vocabulary. It has returned us to early modern understandings of lively machines, animal spirits, subtle matter, an unimaginably vast interstellar universe, fragile bodies, forceful passions, and the need to model our attentiveness on the rhythms of the natural world. Descartes mobilises all these alliances. If what it means to think ecologically is to bring to the table a complex sense of our relationship with our shared planet, then he indisputably does this. And if he does this – if *even he* does this, while pursuing metaphysical and scientific certainty – then this surely shows how urgent and necessary the ecological imperative is. We *have* to think about humans as closely intertwined with geology and ambience and place and space, our subjectivities placed out of centre, our forms of agency relational. We cannot not.

Writing from within the 'permanent crisis' in humanities teaching, from a position of 'disenchantment' (Reitter and Wellmon 2021), it does not feel too extreme to see Descartes as a particularly vital test case. There seems a pressing need, at this moment, to divert current and future students away from a couple of ideas: that the seventeenth century plunges us backwards into a nightmare of human exceptionalism, and that to value Descartes is to be complicit in a realm of exploitative autonomy. These simplifications are harmful. If, truly, we wish to commit to the widest flourishing of the earth, and to combat any modern impulse to maintain privileges at the expense of other human or non-human beings, then understanding the simultaneous fragility and scrupulousness of this body of work is a good place to start. If we remove Descartes as 'bugbear' from our arguments and replace that with Descartes as 'object of study', then we can perceive an uneasy push and pull, in the seventeenth century as today, between rationalism and imagination, between the meeting of human needs and a respect for our environs. Studying those tensions in the past – in all their local, messy, and sometimes unpleasant detail – gives us a new set of resources, as we try and construct a humane ethical framework for the future. Early modern texts, in their own complex figurations of place and space, 'allow us to pay attention to our "home-right-here"' – an alternative model to our 'veneration of "wild-places-out-there"' (Mackenzie 2022, 99–100).

I have suggested that Descartes's world, and that of his contemporaries, is one of never-predictable bereavement, formation, dissolution, and eruption. He attends to times that stretch before and beyond the modern – from the ancient past to the possible collapse of our solar system in the future. He switches scale constantly, from the boundaries and firesides of the individual to the extended substance that connects all bodies. In his scientific work, he traces out the motion of organic change, as particles vibrate, stars rotate, and matter coalesces. His discussion of how the animal spirits function, their flows and channels and directive force, simultaneously explains and discharges the category of the human. He activates and reactivates the liveliness of mechanism, and attunes to the resonances of the world around. Revisiting Descartes, and especially Descartes and the non-human, allows us to think both with and in the world we inhabit.

References

Primary Sources

Arnauld, A. (2020). *Lettres*. In J. Lesaulnier, F. Pouge-Bellais and A.-C. Volongo (eds.), *Œuvres complètes. Tome 1.*, 3 vols., vol. 2. Paris: Classiques Garnier.

Astell, M. (1694). *A Serious Proposal to the Ladies, for the Advancement of their True and Greatest Interest: By a Lover of Her Sex*. London: Wilkin.

Bacon, F. (1857–1874). 'The Great Instauration'. In J. Spedding, R. Ellis, and D. Heath (eds.), *The Works of Francis Bacon*, 14 vols., vol. 4. London: Longmans & Co., pp. 1–38.

Bacon, R. (1859). *Opus tertium*, in *Opera quaedam hactenus inedita*. Ed. J. S. Brewer. London: Longman, Green, Longman and Roberts.

Bartholin, T. (1655). *Defensio vasorum lacteorum et lymphaticorum adversus Joannem Riolanum*. Copenhagen: Georg Holst.

Daniel, G. (1690). *Voyage du monde de Descartes*. Paris: Veuve de Simon Bénard.

Daniel, G. (1692). *A Voyage to the World of Cartesius Written Originally in French, and now Translated into English*. London, Thomas Bennet. Consulted in *ProQuest*, Early English Books Online. https://ezp.lib.cam.ac.uk/login?url=https://www.proquest.com/books/voyage-world-cartesius-written-originally-french/docview/2240924779/se-2.

Descartes, R. (1985). *The Philosophical Writings of Descartes*. Ed., J. Cottingham, R. Stoothoff, and D. Murdoch. 2 vols. Cambridge: Cambridge University Press.

Descartes, R. (1991). *The Philosophical Writings of Descartes, vol. III, The Correspondence*. Ed. and trans. J. Cottingham, R. Stoothoff, D. Murdoch and A. Kenny. Cambridge: Cambridge University Press.

Descartes, R. (1996). *Œuvres de Descartes*. Ed. C. Adam and P. Tannery, new ed., 11 vols. Paris: Léopold Cerf; repr. Paris: Vrin.

Descartes, R. (1998). *The World and Other Writings*. Ed. and trans. S. Gaukroger. Cambridge: Cambridge University Press.

Descartes, R. (2006). *A Discourse on the Method*. Trans. I. Maclean. Oxford: World's Classics.

Descartes, R. (2008). *Meditations on First Philosophy: With Selections from the Objections and Replies*. Trans. M. Moriarty. Oxford: World's Classics.

Descartes, R. (2015). *The Passions of the Soul, and Other Late Philosophical Writings*. Trans. M. Moriarty. Oxford: World's Classics.

Descartes, R. (2024a). *Œuvres I, II. Nouvelle édition préparée par Jean-Marie Beyssade et publiée sous la direction de Denis Kambouchner. Choix de lettres par Jean-Robert Armogathe.* Paris: Gallimard (Pléiade).

Descartes, R. (2024b). *The Complete Correspondence in English Translation, Volume I. From the Early Years to the Discourse on Method, 1619–1638.* Oxford: Oxford University Press.

Digby, Sir K. (1644). *Two Treatises: In the One of Which, the Nature of Bodies; in the Other, the Nature of Man's Soule, Is Looked into: In Way of Discovery of the Immortality of Reasonable Soules.* Paris: Gilles Blaizot.

Donne, J. (1919). *Sermons: Selected Passages, with an Essay by Logan Pearsall Smith.* Oxford: Clarendon Press.

Evelyn, J. (2015). *The Diary of John Evelyn.* Ed. A. Dobson. Cambridge: Cambridge University Press.

Fontaine, N. (1738). *Mémoires pour servir à l'histoire de Port-Royal.* Cologne: Aux dépens de la Compagnie.

Greene, R. (1958). 'The Honourable History of Friar Bacon and Friar Bungay'. In A. Thorndike (ed.), *Minor Elizabethan Drama*, vol. 2. London: Everyman, pp. 163–226.

Hooke, R. (1665). *Micrographia, or Some Physiological Descriptions of Minute Bodies Made by Magnifying Glasses.* London: J. Martyn and J. Allestry.

La Fontaine, J. de (1923). *Fables.* Eds. E. Pilon and F. Dauphin. Paris: Garnier Frères.

Malebranche, N. (1945). De la recherche de la vérité, *où l'on traite de la nature de l'esprit de l'homme, et de l'usage qu'il en doit faire pour éviter les erreurs dans les sciences.* Ed. G. Rodis-Lewis. 2 vols. Paris: Vrin.

Montaigne, M. de. (1999). *Essais*, Ed. Pierre Villey. Paris: PUF.

Montaigne, M. de. (2003). *Essays.* In D. Frame (Trans.). *The Complete Works of Montaigne.* New York: Knopf (Everyman).

Pascal, B. (1962). *Pensées.* Ed. L. Lafuma. Paris: Seuil.

Poliziano, A. (2006). *Letters*, vol. 1, books 1–4. Ed. and trans. S. Butler. Cambridge, MA: Harvard University Press (I Tatti Renaissance Library).

Poisson, N.-J. (1670). *Commentaires ou remarques sur la Méthode de René Descartes.* Vendôme, S. Hip.

Poulain de la Barre, F. (2021). *De l'égalité des deux sexes, De l'éducation des dames, De l'excellence des hommes.* Ed. M.-F. Pellegrin. Paris: Vrin.

Poussin, N. (1964). *Lettres et propos sur l'art.* Ed. A. Blunt. Paris: Hermann.

Scudéry, M. de (2022). *Histoire de deux caméléons, suivi de Description anatomique de Claude Perrault*, Eds. A. Volpilhac, A. Herrel and T. Hoquet. Vincennes: Thierry Marchaisse.

Trublet, N. C. J. (1759). *Mémoires pour servir à l'histoire de la vie et des ouvrages de Mr. de Fontenelle tirés du Mercure de France 1756, 1757 et 1758*. Amsterdam: Marc Michel Rey. 2nd ed.

Valla, L. (1973). *Laurentii Valle Gesta Ferdinandi regis Araganorum*. Ed. Ottavio Besomi. Padova: Antenore.

Secondary Sources

Alfani, G. (2013). 'Plague in Seventeenth-Century Europe and the Decline of Italy: An Epidemiological Hypothesis'. *European Review of Economic History* 17.4, pp. 408–430, https://doi.org/10.1093/ereh/het013.

Allen Shotwell, R. (2013). 'The Revival of Vivisection in the Sixteenth Century'. *Journal of the History of Biology* 46.2, pp. 171–197, https://doi .org/10.1007/s10739-012-9326-8.

Andrault, R. (2022). 'Tirer sur la corde'. In M. Bedon and J.-L. Lantoine (eds.), *L'homme et la brute au XVIIe siècle*. Lyons: ENS Éditions, pp. 83–104, https://doi.org/10.4000/books.enseditions.39937.

Andrault, R. (2024). *Le Fer ou le feu. Penser la douleur après Descartes*. Paris: Garnier.

Ariew, R., J. Cottingham, and T. Sorell. (1998). *Descartes'* Meditations*: Background Source Materials*. Cambridge: Cambridge University Press.

Bedini, S. A. (1980). 'The Mechanical Clock and the Scientific Revolution'. In K. Maurice and O. Mayr (eds.), *The Clockwork Universe: German Clocks and Automata, 1550–1650*, exh. cat., Washington, DC: Smithsonian Institution, pp. 21–22.

Bennett, J. (2010). *Vibrant Matter: A Political Ecology of Things*. Durham: Duke University Press.

Bergin, J. (2001). *The Seventeenth Century*. Oxford: Oxford University Press (Short Oxford History of Europe).

Birch, J. (2024). *The Edge of Sentience: Risk and Precaution in Humans, Other Animals, and AI* (Oxford, 2024; online ed., Oxford Academic, 19 July 2024), https://doi.org/10.1093/9780191966729.001.0001.

Bitbol-Hespériès, A. (1990). *Le Principe de vie chez Descartes*. Paris: Vrin.

Blackburn, S. (1999). *Think: A Compelling Introduction to Philosophy*. Oxford: Oxford University Press.

Blackwell, R. J. (1991). *Galileo, Bellarmine and the Bible*. Notre Dame: Notre Dame University Press.

Borlik, Todd A. (2009). The Chameleon's Dish: Shakespeare and the Omnivore's Dilemma. *Early English Studies* 2 *ProQuest*. 14 January 2025.

Cassin, B. (ed.) (2014). *Dictionary of Untranslatables: A Philosophical Lexicon*. Trans. S. Rendall, C. Hubert, J. Mehlman, N. Stein, and M. Syrotinski, trans. ed. E. Apter, J. Lezra, and M. Wood. Princeton: Princeton University Press.

Clark, T. (2019). *The Value of Ecocriticism*. Cambridge: Cambridge University Press.

Clarke, D. (2003). 'Pascal's Philosophy of Science'. In N. Hammond (ed.), *The Cambridge Companion to Pascal*. Cambridge: Cambridge University Press, pp. 102–122.

Cottingham, J. (1978). '"A Brute to the Brutes?" Descartes's Treatment of Animals'. *Philosophy* 53.206, pp. 551–559.

Cottingham, J. (1985). 'Cartesian Trialism'. *Mind* 94.374, pp. 218–230.

Crowley, M. (2022). *Accidental Agents: Ecological Politics Beyond the Human*. New York: Columbia University Press.

Damasio, A. (1994). *Descartes' Error: Emotion, Reason and the Human Brain*. London: Picador.

Dear, P. (1998). 'A Mechanical Microcosm: Bodily Passions, Good Manners, and Cartesian Mechanism'. In C. Lawrence and S. Shapin (eds.), *Science Incarnate: Historical Embodiments of Natural Knowledge*. Chicago: University of Chicago Press, pp. 51–82.

Deaux, G. (1969). *The Black Death, 1347*. New York: Weybright and Talley.

Derrida, J. (2008). *The Animal that Therefore I am*. Ed. M.-L. Mallet. Trans. D. Wills. New York: Fordham University Press.

Dickey, S. (1991). 'Shakespeare's Mastiff Comedy'. *Shakespeare Quarterly* 42.3, pp. 255–275.

Faraday, C. J. (2019). 'Tudor Time Machines: Clocks and Watches in English Portraits c.1530–c.1630'. *Renaissance Studies* 33.2, pp. 239–266.

Ferry, L. (1995). *The New Ecological Order*. Trans. C. Volk. Chicago: University of Chicago Press.

Finch-Race, D. A. and S. Posthumus (eds.) (2017). *French Ecocriticism: From the Early Modern Period to the Twenty-first Century*. Frankfurt: Peter Lang.

French, R. (1999). *Dissection and Vivisection in the European Renaissance*. Brookfield: Ashgate.

Garrard, G. (2011). *Ecocriticism*. Hoboken: Taylor & Francis.

Garrard, G. (ed.) (2014). *The Oxford Handbook of Ecocriticism*. New York: Oxford University Press.

Gaukroger, S. (2002). *Descartes' System of Natural Philosophy*. Cambridge: Cambridge University Press.

Gaukroger, S. (ed.) (2006). *The Blackwell Guide to Descartes's Meditations*. Oxford: Blackwell.

Gilby, E. (2019). *Descartes's Fictions: Reading Philosophy with Poetics*. Oxford: Oxford University Press.

Glatter K. A. and P. Finkelman (2021). 'History of the Plague: An Ancient Pandemic for the Age of COVID-19'. *The American Journal of Medicine* 134.2, pp. 176–181, https://doi.org/10.1016/j.amjmed.2020.08.019.

Glazebrook, T. (2023). 'Ecofeminism'. In F. Maggino (ed.), *Encyclopedia of Quality of Life and Well-Being* Research. Cham: Springer International Publishing, ebook (pdf).

Gontier, T. (1991). 'Les animaux-machines chez Descartes: modèle ou réalité?' *Corpus: Revue de philosophie* 16, pp. 3–16.

Gontier, T. (2001). 'Le corps humain est-il une machine? Automatisme et biopouvoir chez Descartes'. *Revue philosophique de la France et de l'étranger* 2001.1, pp. 27–53.

Gontier, T. (2010). 'Descartes et les animaux-machines: une réhabilitation'. In J.-L. Guichet (ed.), *De l'animal-machine à l'âme des machines*. Paris: Éditions de la Sorbonne, pp. 25–44. https://doi.org/10.4000/books.psorbonne.17517.

Goodbody, A. (2013). 'Ecocritical Theory: Romantic Roots and Impulses from Twentieth-Century European Thinkers'. In L. Westling (ed.), *The Cambridge Companion to Literature and the Environment*. Cambridge: Cambridge University Press, pp. 61–74.

Goul, P., and P. J. Usher (eds.) (2020). *Early Modern Écologies: Beyond English Ecocriticism*. Amsterdam: Amsterdam University Press.

Grafton, A. (2023). *Magus: The Art of Magic from Faustus to Agrippa*. London: Allen Lane.

Gray, J. (2002). *Straw Dogs: Thoughts on Humans and Other Animals*. London: Granta.

Harrison, P. (2007). *The Fall of Man and the Foundations of Science*. Cambridge: Cambridge University Press.

Hatfield, G. (2006). 'The Cartesian Circle'. In S. Gaukroger (ed.), *The Blackwell Guide to Descartes's* Meditations. Oxford: Blackwell, pp. 122–241.

Hatfield, G. (2008). 'Animals'. In J. Carriero and J. Broughton (eds.), *Companion to Descartes*. Oxford: Blackwell. pp. 404–425.

Heise, U. K. (2006). 'The Hitchhiker's Guide to Ecocriticism'. *PMLA/ Publications of the Modern Language Association of America* 121, pp. 503–516.

Hopkins, R. (2018). Interview with Robert Macfarlane: 'The Metaphors We Use Deliver us Hope, or they Foreclose Possibility'. www.resilience.org/

stories/2018-06-05/robert-macfarlane-the-metaphors-we-use-deliver-us-hope-or-they-foreclose-possibility/.

James, S. (1997). *Passion and Action: The Emotions in Seventeenth-Century Philosophy.* Oxford: Oxford University Press.

James, S. (ed.) (2021). *Life and Death in Early Modern Philosophy.* Oxford: Oxford University Press.

Kambouchner, D. (1995). *L'Homme des passions. Commentaires sur Descartes.* 2 vols. Paris: Albin Michel.

Kambouchner, D. (2015). *Descartes n'a pas dit [. . .].* Paris: Les Belles Lettres.

Kambouchner, D. (2019). 'Descartes and the Passions'. In S. Nadler, T. M. Schmaltz, and D. Antoine-Mahut (eds.), *The Oxford Handbook of Descartes and Cartesianism.* Oxford: Oxford University Press, pp. 193–208.

Kambouchner, D. (2023). *La question Descartes.* Paris: Gallimard.

Kambouchner, D. (2024). 'Descartes and the Ownership of the World'. *Anuario Filosófico* 57/2, pp. 229–244, https://doi.org/10.15581/009.57.2.003.

Kang, M. (2011). *Sublime Dreams of Living Machines: The Automaton in the European Imagination.* Cambridge, MA: Harvard University Press.

Kang, M. (2017). 'The Mechanical Daughter of René Descartes: The Origin and History of an Intellectual Fable'. *Modern Intellectual History* 14.3, pp. 633–660, https://doi.org/10.1017/S147924431600024X.

Kerman, S. (2023). 'Musical and Automaton Clocks and Watches: Sound and Motion in Time-Telling Devices'. In A. Turner, J. Nye, and J. Betts (eds.), *A General History of Horology*, Oxford, 2022; online ed., Oxford Academic, 22 June 2023, https://doi.org/10.1093/oso/9780198863915.003.0010.

Krell, J. (2012). 'Michel Serres, Luc Ferry, and the Possibility of a Natural Contract'. In J. Persels (ed.), *The Environment in French and Francophone Literature and Film.* Leiden: Brill, pp. 1–13.

Landes, D. S. (1983). *Revolution in Time: Clocks and the Making of the Modern World.* Cambridge, MA: The Belknap Press.

Latour, B. (1993). *We Have Never Been Modern*, trans. C. Porter. Cambridge, MA: Harvard University Press.

Latour, B. (2004). *Politics of Nature: How to Bring the Sciences into Democracy.* trans. C. Porter. Cambridge, MA: Harvard University Press.

Latour, B. (2005). *Reassembling the Social: An Introduction to Actor-Network-Theory.* Oxford: Oxford University Press.

Le Roy Ladurie, E. (2004). *Histoire humaine et comparée du climat, vol. I: Canicules et glaciers (XIIIe–XVIIIe siècle).* Paris: Fayard.

Lewis, S. L. and M. A. Maslin. (2015). 'Defining the Anthropocene'. *Nature* 519, pp. 171–180.

Linzey, A. (2016). *Christianity and the Rights of Animals*. Eugene: Wipf and Stock Publishers. 2nd ed.

Macfarlane, R. (2016). Generation Anthropocene: How Humans Have Altered the Planet for Ever. *The Guardian*, Friday 1 April 2016, www.theguardian.com/books/2016/apr/01/generation-anthropocene-altered-planet-for-ever.

Mackenzie, L. (2022). 'Revisiting Places: Can We Still Be Early Modern? Keynote Address, Early Modern French Conference of the Society for Early Modern French Studies, 5–7 July 2022, St Andrews'. *Early Modern French Studies* 45.2, pp. 98–113, https://doi.org/10.1080/20563035.2022.2152301.

Merchant, C. (1980). *The Death of Nature: Women, Ecology, and the Scientific Revolution*. San Francisco: Harper Collins.

Merchant, C. (2010). *Ecological Revolution: Nature, Gender and Science in New England*. Chapel Hill: University of North Carolina Press. 2nd ed.

Midgley, M. (1983). *Animals and Why They Matter: A Journey around the Species Barrier*. Harmondsworth: Penguin.

Moriarty, M. (2015). 'Montaigne and Descartes'. In P. Desan (ed.), *The Oxford Handbook of Montaigne*. Oxford: Oxford University Press, pp. 347–364.

Morton, T. (2007). *Ecology without Nature: Rethinking Environmental Aesthetics*. Cambridge, MA: Harvard University Press.

Morton, T. (2016). *Dark Ecology: For a Logic of Future Coexistence*. New York: Columbia University Press.

Morton, T. (2018). *Being Ecological*. London: Pelican.

Ngai, S. (2005). *Ugly Feelings*. Harvard, MA: Harvard University Press.

Oelze, A. (2018). *Animal Rationality: Later Medieval Theories 1250–1350*. Leiden: Brill.

Parker, G. (ed.) (1987). *The Thirty Years' War*. London: Routledge, 2nd ed.

Parker, G. (2008). 'Crisis and Catastrophe: The Global Crisis of the Seventeenth Century Reconsidered'. *The American Historical Review* 113.4, pp. 1053–1079, https://doi.org/10.1086/ahr.113.4.1053.

Pellegrin, M. F. (2019). 'Cartesianism and Feminism'. In S. Nadler, T. M. Schmaltz, and D. Antoine-Mahut (eds.), *The Oxford Handbook of Descartes and Cartesianism*. Oxford: Oxford University Press, pp. 565–579, https://doi.org/10.1093/oxfordhb/9780198796909.013.35.

Persels, J. (ed.) (2012). *The Environment in French and Francophone Literature and Film*. Leiden: Brill.

Plumwood, V. (1993). *Feminism and the Mastery of Nature*. New York: Routledge.

Pollan M. (2006). *The Omnivore's Dilemma: A Natural History of Four Meals*. London: Penguin Books.

Posthumus, S. (2007). 'Translating Ecocriticism: Dialoguing with Michel Serres'. *Reconstruction* Special Issue: *Eco-Cultures: Culture Studies and the Environment* 7.2, pp. 1–24. http://reconstruction.digitalodu.com/Issues/072/contents072.shtml.

Posthumus, S. (2019). Is *écocritique* Still Possible? *French Studies* 73.4, pp. 598–607.

Rathery, E. J. B and Boutron, P.-A. (eds.) (1873). *Mlle de Scudéry, sa vie et sa correspondence avec un choix de ses poèmes*. Paris: Techener.

Reitter, P. and C. Wellmon. (2021). *Permanent Crisis: The Humanities in a Disenchanted Age*. Chicago: University of Chicago Press.

Riskin, J. (2016). *The Restless Clock: A History of the Centuries-Long Argument over What Makes Living Things Tick*. Chicago: University of Chicago Press.

Roger, J. (1982). 'The Cartesian Model and its Role in Eighteenth-Century Theory of the Earth'. In T. M. Lennon, J. M. Nicholas, and J. W. Davis (eds.), *Problems of Cartesianism*. Montreal: McGill-Queen's University Press, pp. 95–112, https://doi.org/10.1515/9780773563964.

Secord, J. A. (2023). Inventing the Scientific Revolution. *Isis* 114.1, pp. 50–76.

Serres, M. (1995). *The Natural Contract*. Trans. E. MacArthur and W. Paulson. Ann Arbor: University of Michigan Press.

Shapin, S. (1996). *The Scientific Revolution*. Chicago: University of Chicago Press.

Singer, P. (1975). *Animal Liberation: A New Ethics for Our Treatment of Animals*. London: Cape.

Stoffel, M., C. Corona and F. Ludlow, et al. (2022) 'Climatic, Weather, and Socio-economic Conditions Corresponding to the Mid-17th-century Eruption Cluster'. *Climate of the Past* 18, pp. 1083–1108, https://doi.org/10.5194/cp-18-1083-2022.

Taylor, C. (1989). *Sources of the Self: The Making of Modern Identity*. Cambridge: Cambridge University Press.

Taylor, H. (2021). Antoinette Deshoulières's Cat: Polemical Equivocation in Salon Verse. *Romanic Review* 112.3, pp. 452–469.

Usher, P. J. (2016). Untranslating the Anthropocene. *Diacritics* 44.3, pp. 56–76.

Vermij, R. (2023). 'Florentius Schuyl and the Origin of the Beast-Machine Controversy'. *History of European Ideas* 50.2, pp. 193–210, https://doi.org/10.1080/01916599.2023.2250794.

Warren, K. J. (2000). *Ecofeminist Philosophy: A Western Perspective on What it Is and Why it Matters*. Oxford: Rowman & Littlefield.

Wee, C. (2001). 'Cartesian Environmental Ethics'. *Environmental Ethics* 23.3, pp. 275–286.

Westling, L. (ed.) (2013). *The Cambridge Companion to Literature and the Environment*. Cambridge: Cambridge University Press.

Wilson, P. H. (2009). *The Thirty Years War: Europe's Tragedy*. Harvard, MA: Harvard University Press.

Wilson-Lee, E. (2025). *The Grammar of Angels: A Search for the Magical Powers of Sublime Language*. London: William Collins.

Acknowledgements

This Element has its origins in a cross-faculty Transhistorical Humanities seminar that I attended in Cambridge in March 2024, convened by Tobias Barnett and Carlos Iglesias-Crespo with the support of the Faculty of Modern and Medieval Languages and Linguistics. Entitled 'Cognition Across Time', the session featured papers from Ian James and Heather Webb, and a response from Tim Chesters. Audience discussion turned to Descartes, and there was some agreement about his (let us say) emblematic status in the modern environmental humanities. The open and generous interest in seventeenth-century perspectives inspired this project.

Reading Descartes has trained me to think in new and different ways, and so has engaging with the wealth of contemporary criticism on his philosophy. As with my previous work, I have been enormously influenced by the recalibrations, retranslations, editions, summaries, and careful footnotes of Roger Ariew, Erik-Jan Bos, Susan James, Denis Kambouchner, Michael Moriarty, and Theo Verbeek among others. I would like to thank my current PhD student, Carrie Heusinkveld, whose work on the dramatist Jean Racine is always beautifully articulated from an ecocritical perspective, and who has helped to deepen my own thinking on the environmental early modern. And I would also like to thank, alongside the helpful anonymous readers for the press, those friends and colleagues who saw this work in draft form: Tim Chesters, Emma Claussen, Nick Hammond, Denis Kambouchner, Ian James, Tim Lewens, John Lyons, Michael Moriarty, Annalisa Nicholson, Sura Qadiri, and Helena Taylor. Finally, my thanks to my CUP editors, Louise Westling, Serenella Iovino, and Timo Maran: I am very grateful that this work has found a home in their series.

Cambridge Elements ☰

Environmental Humanities

About the Series

The environmental humanities is a new transdisciplinary complex of approaches to the embeddedness of human life and culture in all the dynamics that characterize the life of the planet. These approaches reexamine our species' history in light of the intensifying awareness of drastic climate change and ongoing mass extinction. To engage this reality, Cambridge Elements in Environmental Humanities builds on the idea of a more hybrid and participatory mode of research and debate, connecting critical and creative fields.

Cambridge Elements

Environmental Humanities

Elements in the Series

A full series listing is available at: www.cambridge.org/EIEH

For EU product safety concerns, contact us at Calle de José Abascal, 56–1°, 28003 Madrid, Spain or eugpsr@cambridge.org.

www.ingramcontent.com/pod-product-compliance
Ingram Content Group UK Ltd.
Pitfield, Milton Keynes, MK11 3LW, UK
UKHW020421250726
13967UKWH00007B/2763

* 9 7 8 1 0 0 9 6 1 7 1 4 7 *